Changing Times

Almanac and Digest of
Kansas City's Gay and Lesbian History

edited by
David W. Jackson

45th Anniversary Commemorative

Kansas City, Missouri
2011

Jackson, David W. (1969-)
    Changing Times: Almanac and Digest of Kansas City's Gay and Lesbian History
        162 p.   cm.
    Includes bibliographical references and index.

        ISBN-13: 978-0970430847 (The Orderly Pack Rat)
        ISBN: 0970430841

First Edition, October 2011.

1. Gay men—United States—History—20th century. 2. Lesbians—United States—History—20th century. 3. Bisexuals—United States--History—20th century. 4. Transgender people—United States—History—20th century. 5. Homosexuality—United States—History—20th century. 6. Gay liberation movement—United States—History. 7. Gay community—History. 8. Almanacs, American. I. Jackson, David W., (1969-). II. Title.

Published by:
The Orderly Pack Rat
Kansas City, Missouri

Benefitting the Gay and Lesbian Archive of Mid-America (GLAMA)

Available at:
amazon.com   createspace.com   abe.com

TABLE OF CONTENTS

INTRODUCTION

The 'gay liberation' movement catapulted in Kansas City in February 1966, when the National Planning Conference of Homophile Organizations (NPCHO) was established to form a national coalition of gay and lesbian leaders. This first-ever, truly national coalition of lesbian, gay, bisexual and transgender (LGBT) leaders decided to meet at the Hotel State (aka The Stats) (northeast corner of 12th and Wyandotte; since demolished) in downtown Kansas City, Missouri.

In 2011, we recognize the 45th anniversary of this historic local event with national impact.

Changing Times pays homage to Phyllis Fay (Forney) Shafer, the extremely proud mother of her gay son, Drew Shafer, who unwittingly became one of Kansas City's 'gay liberation' activists. Mrs. Shafer exemplifies the kind of mother any youth would relish ... especially for LGBT children who to this day in 2011 face harassment, bias, and discrimination because of their gender orientation.

Mrs. Shafer possessed the gifts of hindsight and optimistic foresight to see that, "Times, they are a changin'." She noted that homophobic people (like Anita Bryant) are oftentimes the best proponents for LGBT individuals and their quest for equal rights. She believed that Bryant did more good than bad in the long-run for gays and lesbians. And the local *Kansas City Times* backed up her argument on June 15, 1977, when it reported, *"The greater threat to this society, which struggles toward justice for all, is not the ordinary homosexual; it is*

the Anita Bryant's who catch up so many gullible and unsophisticated Americans in their messianic madness."

In the scrapbooks she created, you can see the changing times in thought and feeling for and against LGBT individuals, and the challenges they have faced and freedoms they sought and fought for DECADES ... from fair employment in the U. S. military to marriage equality for *every* loving, committed couple regardless of gender.

Presented here is my first attempt to share some meaningful history relating to Kansas City's LGBT community.

To keep the concept simple, I started by 'data mining' everything I could find about the subject in a variety of venues and formats in order to construct a working (i.e., changing) timeline of LGBT-related events, activities, benchmarks and milestone moments. Material was abstracted from newspaper and magazine articles; online databases and websites; historical collections; and, even personal recollections.

While focusing on local, Kansas City-area happenings, regional and national events were added for context; and, a couple entries were inserted for pure humor.

To diversify the content and introduce a digest component to this compendium, a couple local history-related articles round out this first edition of *Changing Times*.

Look for expanded offerings and images in future editions. The almanac and digest format should afford the opportunity to continue chronicling life as it continues to change for LGBT individuals in and around Kansas City.

Enjoy,
David W. Jackson
Kansas City, Missouri

> *"Make you the world a bit better*
> *or more beautiful because you have lived in it."*
> --Welmoet Tideman, grandmother of Edward Bok

CHAPTER 1

Kansas City's LGBT Changing Timeline
(with regional/global context in un-bold text)

1812   **Missouri becomes a territory and adopts the sodomy laws of the Louisiana Territory.** The state removed the sodomy laws in 2006.[1]

1855   **Kansas Territorial Legislature adopts sodomy laws. Kansas has yet to repeal them, even though they became inactive in 2003 by Supreme Court ruling (Lawrence v. Texas that decreed laws prohibiting sodomy are unconstitutional)**

1869   The term " Homosexualität " appears in print for the first time in a German pamphlet written by Karl-Maria Kertbeny (1824-1882).[2]

1870   **David W. Jackson's earliest ancestor emigrates and settles in Kansas City. Edward Bischofsberger lived with his young family on *Gay Street* that ran south from Indepencence Avenue. *Gay Street* was eventually lost to history when it was re-named *Charlotte*, which at that time, ran south from Levee (near the Missouri River) to Independence Avenue.**[3]

1882   **Oscar Wilde performed to a sold-out audience at the Coates Opera House. According to Felicia Londre's book, *The Enchanted Years of the Stage*,**

Kansas Citians had never seen such a flamboyant character dressed in "purple velvet breeches with knee buckles, black silk stockings, cutaway coat, white neck scarf with diamonds and long, center-parted hair."[4] (April 17)

1890s   The "Gay 90s" were fun and all ... even decadent; but, the term doesn't mean what you think.

1903   New York City police conduct the first recorded raid on a gay bathhouse.[5] (February 21)

1910   Emma Goldman first begins speaking publicly in favor of homosexual rights.[6]

1913   The word "faggot" is first used in print in reference to gays in a vocabulary of criminal slang published in Portland, Oregon: "All the fagots [sic] (sissies) will be dressed in drag at the ball tonight."[7]

1913   President Roosevelt sends a message to boys of America, "a homely little talk on the value of manliness." He said, "I have no use for mollycoddles, I have no use for timid boys, for the 'sissie' type of boys." This was published in the December issue of "Boy's Life," the magazine of the Boy Scouts of America.[8] (November 26)

1920   The word "gay" is used for the first time in reference to homosexuals in the Underground.[9]

GAY

1923   The word "fag" is first used in print in Nels Anderson's The Hobo: "Fairies or Fags are men or boys who exploit sex for profit."[10]

1924   *The Society for Human Rights* in Chicago becomes the country's earliest known gay rights organization. Panama, Paraguay and Peru legalize homosexuality.[11]

1925   Ma Rainey is arrested for taking part in an orgy at home involving women in her chorus. Bessie Smith bailed her out of jail. Ma Rainey's album cover "Prove to Me Blues," a monologue about women who love women, showed a women who looked like Rainey, in a hat, tie and jacket talking to a flapper.

               Rainey--who was in trouble with the police several times for her lesbian behavior--performed at the Lincoln Theater in Kansas City's Jazz District at 18th and Lydia. Many of the Harlem Renaissance's key literary and musical performers were homo- or bisexual, including Alberta Hunter (who also performed at Lincoln Theater). Advertised largely by word of mouth to those "in the life," Queer nightlife thrived in Harlem. Greenwich Village and Harlem were the city's main areas that countenanced homosexual gatherings. **Through the 1930s and into the post-World War II years, gay cabaret, based largely on female impersonation, survived in Kansas City (and in a circuit that included Chicago, New Orleans, Miami, San Francisco, Seattle, and other cities).**[12]

1929   The Reichstag Committee votes to repeal Paragraph 175. The Nazis' rise to power prevents the implementation of the vote.[13] (October 16)

1937   The first use of the pink triangle badge (use your highlighter to color this pink) to identify male prisoners sent to Nazi concentration camps for being suspected of being homosexual.[14]

1948   Alfred Kinsey publishes *Sexual Behavior in the Human Male*, a groundbreaking study which broaches topics of homosexuality and bisexuality previously undiscussed.[15]

1950   A small group of men led by Harry Hay and Chuck Rowland meet in Los Angeles to form what would become later that month the *Mattachine Society*, named after Medieval French secret societies of masked men who, through their anonymity, were empowered to criticize ruling monarchs with impunity. *Mattachine Society* became the country's first national gay rights organization.[16] (November 11)

1952   ONE National Gay and Lesbian Archives founded.[17] (November 29)

1953   President Dwight D. Eisenhower issues an executive order [Exec. Order No. 10450, 3 C.F.R. 936, 938 (1953)] [effective May 27, 1953] adding "sexual perversion" as a ground for investigation under the federal loyalty-security program, and barred gay men and lesbians from all federal jobs. Many state and local governments and private corporations followed suit. The FBI began a surveillance program against homosexuals.[18] (April)

1955   *Daughters of Bilitis*, a lesbian organization in San Francisco, founded by Del Martin and Phyllis Lyon, the first national lesbian political and social organization in the United States.[19] (September 21)

1956   **Jeannette Howard Foster, a lesbian librarian who, in the 1940s, started cataloging instances of romance between women, publishes her research in the book, *Sex Variant Women in Literature: A Historical and Quantatative Survey*. "She's now considered one of the foremothers of lesbian literary research," Ross Freese said, "And she lived in Kansas City for about a year on Harrison Boulevard."[20]**

1957   The word "Transsexual" is coined by U.S. physician Harry Benjamin; The Wolfenden Committee's report recommends decriminalizing consensual homosexual behavior between adults in the United Kingdom; Psychologist Evelyn Hooker publishes a study showing that homosexual men are as well adjusted as non-homosexual men, which becomes a major factor in the American Psychiatric Association removing homosexuality from its handbook of disorders in 1973.[21]

Transsexual

| 1960s | New Earth Books, a political bookstore at 47th and Troost, operated by women in the *Women's Liberation Union* (WLU) and the *Lesbian Alliance*. They moved the bookstore to 24 E 39th Street [by the early 1980s, they moved into the Foolkiller Building on the northwest corner of 39th and Main; in the mid-1980s they moved the bookstore to Westport Road but struggled financially. |

New Earth Books changed its name to Phoenix Books, and moved back to its old neighborhood [at 39th and Main]. Phoenix Bookstore was sold to Larry Gilbert in April 1989, and the name changed to Larry's Cards and Gifts.[22]

WLU moved into a house on Charlotte in Hyde Park. The *Lesbian Alliance* ran an information line, monthly dances, and public speakers. WLU proved to be too separatist for many lesbians.

| 1961 | The Colony, an early LGBT watering hole, has "an ad in the phone book in 1961 that said, according to Ross Freese, 'The GAYest bar in Kansas City,'" emphasizing the capitalization. "So the nomenclature was out there — and they weren't afraid to advertise it."[23] |

| 1962 | Illinois repeals its sodomy laws making it the first state in the U.S. to decriminalize homosexuality between two consenting adults in private. The law takes effect in 1962. [Illinois Compiled Statues (720 ILCS 5/12-7.1) (from Ch. 38, par. 12-7.1)][24] |

1964   "A Trick Ain't Always A Treat," the "Original LP record by vaudeville and nightclub performer Rae Bourbon, recorded at the Jewel Box Revue in Kansas City, Missouri.
Jewel Box Lounge was originally located at 3219 Troost Ave., where "femme mimics" or female impersonators sang (i.e., NO lip-synching) and performed comedy routines. Femme mimics also had stage names, as in modern drag, but their names were always preceeded by "Mr." such as, "Mr. Nikki St. Cyr." Many performers chose to go by their real names, not using a stage name. The Jewel Box Lounge, known across the nation as a hot spot for entertainment, later relocated to Main Street (where a Wendy's fast-food restaurant stands today, 2011) (see references in two digest stories apprearing in this volume). Bourbon (aka "Ray Bourbon") started in show business in silent movies and English music hall and, in the 1930s and 40s, was known for his gay themed nightclub review and performances in San Francisco, Los Angeles and many other cities. "A Trick Ain't Always a Treat" was the last of eleven albums Bourbon self-published in the 1950s and 60s."[25]

1965   The first gay rights protests occur in Washington, D.C., and in front of Philadelphia's Independence Hall.[26]

1966   Born out of need for a national coalition of gay and lesbian leaders, the *National Planning Conference of Homophile Organizations* (NPCHO) was established. This first-ever, truly national coalition of LGBT leaders decided to meet at the Hotel State (aka The Stats) (now demolished) in downtown Kansas City, Missouri (Northeast corner of 12th and Wyandotte). It was here that they decided to launch a national campaign to protest the exclusion of homosexuals by the U.S. Military. NPCHO united and formed the *North American Conference of Homophile Organizations* (NACHO, pronounced "NAy-KO").

Kansas City's New Hotel, THE STATS, Twelfth & Wyandotte Sts., KANSAS CITY, MO.

Drew Shafer, Al Greathouse, and Larry Hungerford, were in attendance representing *ONE in Kansas City*. The three joined 36 others from 14 organizations from across the country. Chuck Thompson, of *One, Inc.*, "reported that Drew Shafer of Kansas City has for many years offered his home for use by homosexuals in that city and that the preceding evening 20 of Shafer's friends met and organized a new council of friends of One in Kansas City. Representatives of the council were sitting in the conference as observers." During the afternoon session on February 20, "Shafer reported on the problems facing the newly formed *One, in Kansas City* organization. He stated that while considerable freedom was afforded to homosexual bars and their patrons, in other areas Kansas City shared problems of other localities, such as problems of communication among the homosexual community and police harassment of suspected homosexuals encountered in certain areas of the city. He wished to be recorded as offering the cooperation of his organization with all other homophile organizations, and he expressed the desire that no organization should advance itself at others' expense.... Shafer spoke of social service needs of the Kansas City homosexual community, but he said the group's main problem at that point was in becoming organized. He announced the Kansas City organization's address and asked that his own name not be used in print; he would use a pseudonym [Anthony Sexton] for public use."[27] (February 18-20)

1966   Leaders of *ONE in Kansas City*, decide not to affiliate with *ONE, Inc.*, and the local

organization's name was changed to *Phoenix
Society for Individual Freedom* (originally called the
Society for Individual Rights). "Phoenix Society
served as a model for mid-America in the
development of dialogue with religious, police, and
other community leaders." Two years later, Drew
Shafer led the charge on May 20, 1968, to legally
charter the *Phoenix Society for Individual Freedom.*
"NACHO remained a small, but influential,
element in the gay and lesbian movement over the
next four years.... Probably the most important
long-term effect of the organization's existence was
the opportunity for increasingly radicalized gay
men and lesbians to push for a militant approach
to the common problems they faced."[28] (March)

1966 Don Slater, a full-time gay activist, launches from
his office near the old Universal Studio lots in Los
Angeles, California, "a new crusade in opposition
to the military's policies: *The Committee to Fight
Exclusion of Homosexuals from the Armed Forces.*
He took his cause, the first that concerned gays in
the military, to the *National Planning Conference
of Homophile Organizations* in Kansas City. The
conference included all of forty gay leaders from
fifteen gay groups who agreed that, with the war
growing, the military's ban on gays could be an
issue around which they might mobilize gays. Of
course, hardly anyone took homosexual organizing
very seriously back in the mid-1960s. The
conference received a polite write up in *The New
York Times*, focusing on the military issue...."[29]
(April)

1966   *Phoenix Society for Individual Freedom* debuted the periodical, "The Phoenix: Midwest Homophile Voice," in Kansas City, Missouri, by the organization's founder, Drew Shafer. The publication grew from a newsletter to a regularly published magazine distributed free of charged through Kansas City's gay and lesbian bars. It gained a reputation for being, "well-edited and informative...with a wide circulation." Ronald E. "Ron" Bentley (11 March 1940 – 18 July 1994) was its editor.[30] (May)

1966   At the second *North American Conference of Homophile Organizations* (NACHO), "Ten Days in August," (with proceedings from August 25-27) planned at the Bellevue Hotel, Geary and Taylor Streets, San Francisco, California. *Phoenix Society for Individual Freedom* was scheduled as a participant to present on the "Stimulation of New Organizations," according to tentative agenda items presented by Clarence A. Colwell, Interim Chairman, in his August 5 letter to attendees of the February NACHO Conference. "Anthony Sexton [aka. Drew Shafer], Larry Hungerford, Estel[le] Graham [aka. Mrs. Phyllis Shafer], and Marc Jeffers [aka. William Wynn]," were on Foster Gunnison Jr.'s notes from the conference. Conference organizers decided to form a national clearinghouse of gay and lesbian publications. *Phoenix Society for Individual Freedom* in Kansas City was selected as the home and operator of the "Homopile Clearinghouse." (Phoenix became legally chartered in Illinois on May 20, 1968.)[31] (August 25-27)

1967   "Drew Shafer, President of *Phoenix Society*, was a guest of the KMBC radio station program, ""Assignment Kansas City,"" moderated by Steve Bell. Along with Shafer were Rev. Vann Anderson, Methodist minister, and Dr. George Colom, psychiatrist. This was the first attempt by any radio station in Kansas City to discuss homosexuality, and the first appearance by Shafer in an endeavor to educate via mass media. Shafer explained that Phoenix was ""not a homosexual organization, but rather an organization composed of all types of people working for the improvement of the status of the homosexual."" He also used his own name, which was a daring risk at that time (for instance, he effectively ""came out"" to his employer and fellow co-workers who were tuning in). Shafer's full story, including background history of *Phoenix Society* is explored in a separate article in this digest.[32] (January 10)

1967   "The Phoenix: Midwest Homophile Voice" announced its first Anniversary.[33] (February)

1967   Columbia University student group seeks rights for a student homophile league. They may have been the first to *apply* for such status. The first *sanctioned* group of this kind was in 1969 in Minnesota (see below).[34]

1967 The second *Midwestern Homophile Organizations*, hosted by S.A.M.E. in Rock Island, Illinois. Participants in the Conference were: *SAME; One of Chicago; Mattachine Midwest, Inc.* (of Chicago); and *Phoenix Society*.[35] (August 5-6)

1967 According to the August 1967 issue of the Kansas City-based periodical, "The Phoenix: Midwest Homophile Voice," the organization's headquarters were at 1838 E 49th Street, Kansas City, Missouri. Steve Gingsburg was the honored guest, he being the founder of *PRIDE*, a homophile organization of Los Angeles, California. Vann Anderson was the *Phoenix Society's* chaplain.[36] (August)

1968 Drew Shafer purchased a house at 1333 Linwood (Linwood and The Paseo; no longer standing as of March 1992), and opened *"Phoenix House"* as one of the few Gay  and Lesbian Community Centers in the US...the only one in the Midwest...and the first in Kansas City. It had printing facilities; a lending library; meeting space; and, a hot line. This "three-story residence...soon became a center for recreation and social service for homosexuals who lived in a large area of Kansas and Missouri." Eventually, Shafer and his partner, Mickey Ray, lived on the third floor, rented a room on the second and the organization used the main, first floor and part of the basement as well.[37]

1968   *The Women's Liberation Union* (WLU) moved off the University of Missouri-Kansas City campus and into the *Ecclectic Umbrella* at 38th and Gillham, which also had a childcare cooperative. *The Lesbian Alliance* was added to the WLU collective.[38]

1968   Barbara Grier took over as editor of "The Ladder," having previously contributed to the magazine under a variety of pseudonyms that included Gene Damon, Lennox Strong, and Vern Niven. She made her most significant contribution as a book reviewer, and when she became the editor sought to turn it more professional. It received a smoother layout with more material—the second issue under Grier was 48 pages. Although the headquarters for *The Ladder* were in San Francisco, Grier ran the magazine long-distance from Kansas City. She tripled the subscription rate by removing "lesbian" from the cover to address more feminist issues.[39]

1968   *Kansas City Metropolitan Inter-Church Agency* established a task force on homosexuality. Later, members were asked to serve on the *Metropolitan Police/Community Relations Committee* designed to improve relations between the Kansas City Police Department and minority communities following the civil unrest in 1968.[40] (January)

1968   *The Phoenix Society for Indiviual Freedom* was officially chartered by Drew R. Shafer; Michael Ray; Marc Jeffers; Richard C. Barber (all from 1333 Linwood Blvd, K.C., MO); and, Estelle Graham (1838 E 49th St, K.C., MO). Illinois had removed the sodomy laws in 1961, which is why The *Phoenix Society* incorporated in that state.

Marc Jeffers was a pseudonym for William Wynn (according to Foster Gunnison Jr.'s notes of the August 1966 NACHO Conference in San Francisco, California). Estelle Graham was a pseudonym for Drew Shafer's mother, Mrs. Phyllis Shafer. Chris Gordon was a pseudonym for Dale Martin (his twin sister, Donna, was also with the organization). The registered agent was Paul R. Goldman (100 N LaSalle, Chicago, IL) "to be a not for profit, non-sectarian organization for promoting the understanding and interest of the public in all social variants, especially homosexuals, so that all persons may share equally in the guarantees of democracy under the constitution of the United States of America, regardless of sex or sexual orientation.

This organization intended to work toward the accomplishment of the above by:

1) the education of homosexuals to help them to understand themselves and society, and by aiding in their adjustment to society by sponsoring public discussions on all subjects of concern to homosexuals;

2) the education of the public at large to enable it to accept the homosexual as an individual by the exchange of truth for for prejudice, and by sponsoring public discussion meetings and educational literature regarding the homosexual;

3) furthering knowledge of the homosexual by direct and indirect participation in research projects conducted by recognized experts;

4) investigating the penal code insofar as it concerns homosexuals and by working for beneficial changes in that code by all lawful methods;

5) providing a referral service for the homosexual so that he can have expert professional advice as it is needed;

6) cooperating with all homophile and other such groups which are working for the above purposes;

7) further, to engage in other lawful activities beneficial to the homosexual; and,

8) further, to do any and all things not inconsistent with the above."[41] (May 20)

1968   At the *North American Conference of Homophile Organizations* (NACHO) conference in Chicago, Bill Wayne, *Phoenix Society* President, was elected President of NACHO. Scoop Phillips became clearninghouse director. NACHO adopts the slogan, "Gay is Good."[42] (August)

21

GAY IS GOOD

1968   An amendment to the charter of *The Phoenix Society for Individual Freedom* was filed. (October 6)

1968   "Find Body of Man, 48, in Twin Oaks..." newspaper article announcing the suspected hate-crime murder of Wilbur Colin "Carl" Kuhn and Harold F. Miller ("bar friends" of Phyllis Miller); and, the arrest of Vincent Kenneth Cavallaro.[43] (October 31)

1968   Drew Shafer and Mickey Ray met at a gay pride picnic. Mickey said, *"I'd just left Chicago before the fiasco known as the Democratic Convention got into full swing. My destination was California, with a few stops along the way. (Some guys in Chicago said I ought to make a stop in Kansas City, and that's where I wound up, wondered around, totally irresponsible and looking for opportunities.*

"I'd heard about this organization from a poster I'd seen on the bulletin board of a local Methodist Church. They were having a picnic that Sunday and meeting at what would become known collectively as the Phoenix House, to collect those who would need a ride to the picnic grounds.

"The picnic/party was being held at some member's private property out in the country somewhere.

"I met Drew at that picnic and I wound up living with him from that day until the day he died, 21 years and 29 days later."[44] (September 1)

1968   First services of the *Universal Fellowship of Metropolitan Community Church* in Los Angeles, California, Rev. Troy D. Perry officiating.[45] (October)

1969   "FREE," the first homosexual student group, is formed and sanctioned in the United States at the University of Minnesota.[46]

1969   The Stonewall Riots begin on June 27 for three days, launching the previously quiet gay rights movement into a massive period of social change, with members increasing from hundreds into the thousands in less than a year. The police in New York City raided a Greenwich Village gay bar, the Stonewall Inn. Contrary to expectations, the patrons fought back, provoking three nights of rioting in the area accompanied by the appearance of "gay power" slogans on the buildings. Almost overnight, a massive grassroots gay liberations movement was born.[47] (June 27)

1969   *North American Conference of Homophile Organizations* (NACHO) meeting convened once again in Kansas City, Missouri, this time at the Hotel Bellerive. It was the largest gathering of gay and lesbian activits in Kansas City (up to March 1992). National speakers were featured like Wardell Pomeroy from the Kinsey Institute. Major position papers were drafted on gay and lesbian civil rights and religion, and the "unqualified acceptance by

23

society of homosexuality." Response papers were written to then recent anti-writings by some members of the psychiatric community.[48] (August 5)

1960s (late)
to early 1970s *Sisters in Sin* (SIS) Club, originally an all-male club, was formed in Kansas City with social and philanthropic goals.[49]

1960s (late)
to early 1970s The *Ten Four Hundred Club* (or 10-400 Club), a mixed service organization, was formed in Kansas City, with social and philanthropic goals of assisting individuals in need within the community. The name derived from the address of one of its members.[50]

1960s (late)
to early 1970s *Pete's Bowling League* was formed in Kansas City. Still active as of March 1992.[51]

1970s   **Lesbian Town (in Hyde Park) where women settled because houses were cheap. As Ross Freese explains,** *"They developed skills to support each other — carpentry, plumbing, landscaping — and really started their own community."*[52]

1970   "*North American Conference of Homophile Organizations* (NACHO) members of the Youth Committee decided to abandon a 'respectable' approach to dealing with gay and lesbian issues and agreed to a 'radical manifesto' that they entitled, "The Homophile Movement Must be Radicalized!" and provided a 12-point approach that was, in the end, not adopted by the conference as a whole.[53]

1970   At the sixth *North American Conference on Homophile Organizations* (NACHO) convention and conference at the SIR Center in San Francisco, California, the organization disolved in favor of the new "gay liberation movement."[54] (August)

1970   "In spite of a history of strong leadership and performance, the struggle in 1970 between radicals and reformists resulted in the closing of *Phoenix House* and the [*Phoenix Society for Individual Freedom's*] collapse. *The Society for Individual*

25

Rights, [sic.] at that time the nation's largest homophile group, was torn by an upheaval, largely ideological in nature, within a month after NACHO's demise."[55] (September)

1970   "Gay Liberation: Homosexuals Fighting for Civil Rights" article publishes.[56] (June 29)

1970   "Lawrence 'Gay' Group to Seek Court Action," article about the Lawrence Gay Liberation Front by Carolyn Rortge.[57] (September 11)

1970   *Mid-America Religious Council on Homosexuality* **chartered. The registered agent was Robert C. Downs (900 Walnut, 3rd Fl, K.C., MO).[58] (November 11)**

1970   **"Man Found Slain: First Murder in 5 Years in Lee's Summit," about the suspected hate-crime murder of Robert L. Bowser, 508 South Miller.[59] (December 8)**

1971   *Gay Lib*, a gay campus group, is formed at University of Missouri. The group was endorsed by the Student Senate and the Student-faculty Committee. Still, university officials, including the Dean of Students, vetoed recognition.

1971-73   *The Gay Raiders*, a gay militant group, campaign against television networks to feature and discuss gay people on the air. They disrupt various programs including the CBS Evening News.[60]

1972   Equal Rights Amendment passed and a local woman's movement took shape.[61]

1973   *Metropolitan Community Church of Kansas City* (MCC-KC) (As of 7 Sept 1993, *Spirit of Hope MCC*) began meeting on Sunday mornings in a grove of trees in Volker Park and in peoples' homes. Rev. Vic Adams, Founding Pastor, officiates.[62] (June)

1973   *Metropolitan Community Church of Kansas City* (MCC-KC) (As of 7 Sept 1993, *Spirit of Hope MCC*) chartered. Founder of the MCC in Los Angeles, Rev. Troy D. Perry, visited Kansas City to accept the charter of the *MCC-KC*. *MCC-KC* was the first home for Gay Talk, the Gay and Lesbian crisis line. *MCC-KC* later met at The Asylum and in temporary quarters at *All Souls Unitarian Church*. They dedicated their new space at 4000 Harrison (purchased from First United Pentacostal Church) in October 1976 and held their first sermon there on February 29, 1976.[63] (August 27)

> *Keith Spare said, "I moved to Kansas City in 1973, when MCC was in its infancy and meeting in people's homes.... Somehow I ran into Gerry Young and we organized a group ... for the first gay rights march.*

1973   *Gay Lib* appeals to the University of Missouri but is denied following a ruling by the University Curators decreeing homosexuality to be a sickness and that it should be treated as such. (November)

1973   The American Psychiatric Association removes homosexuality from its Diagnostic and Statistical Manual of Mental Disorders (DSM-II), based largely on the research and advocacy of Evelyn Hooker. A 1976 UP syndicated column about, "Insights: Homosexuality," quoted Dr. Walt Menninger as saying, "The majority of pschiatrists believe that homosexuality, in and of itself, is not an illness.""[64] (December)

1974   **A handful of activists make attempts to start a community center at 3825 Virginia, but lacked the support needed to sustain the few action items being implemented.[65]**

1974   ***Gay People's Union* charted by Glen Strobel (5440 Lydia, K.C., MO). The *Gay People's Union* (GPU) evolved from a student organization at the University of Missouri-Kansas City. GPU rented a house on Forest Street, and operated a gay and lesbian center there for two years. It provided "rap sessions;" social events; and, a "coming out" rite.[66] (March 18)**

1974   ***Gay Community Services* filed its charter with the Missouri Secretary of State.[67] (March 27)**

1974   "Fired Entertainer Loses
Still another Job," article
by J. J. Maloney, about
Tommy Temple, who
was making $575 a week
as the show director at
the Jewel Box Lounge
(and cook at the Tower
Restaurant, across from
the Jewel Box), until,
*"the city ruined me.They
used a part of their liquor
oridnance that said a bar
could not employ a*

*homosexual. The Jewel Box had to fire me. I lost my
home because my income went away."* The ACLU
won his case; but, the Jewel Box had already
closed.[68] (April 7)

1974   Gay Pride Festival in Kansas City featured Rev.
Rob Shivers (MCC-Austin) as the principal
speaker. She later joined *Metropolitan Community
Church of Kansas City* (MCC-KC) as Assistant
Pastor on October 1, 1977.[69] (June)

1974   *Metropolitan Community Church of Kansas City*
(MCC-KC) (As of 7 Sept 1993, *Spirit of Hope MCC*)
welcomed Ronald D. Burcham as Pastor (he left in
November 1976 for Australia).[70] (August)

1975   Governor Milton Shapp of Pennsylvania creates the
first committee to research and report on
discrimination against sexual minorities. One year
later, Governor Shapp issues an executive order

outlawing discrimination against sexual minorities in employment, housing and public accommodation.[71]

1975   *The Ecumenical Foundation* provided education and counseling services. Before they could reach their goal of forming a gay and lesbian professionals' organization, they ceased in 1977.[72]

1975   A small group of gay men began operating a telephone hotline specifically targeted to the gay community of Kansas City. The purpose of the hotline was to answer crisis calls, offer peer counseling and provide information about referrals for services within the community.

1975   Gay Talk crisis line started.[73]

1975   First in a series of three ground-breaking LGBT-related articles is published in the *Kansas City Star*. The first was, "Gay Life: Behind Closed Doors: Gay Vanguard Targeted in Myths, Ordinances," by Diane Stafford and David Zeeck.[74] (April 2)

1975   The second in a series of three articles, "Secret Lives Merge in Gay Bars Amid Aura of Fear," by Diane Stafford and David Zeeck, is published.[75] (April 3)

1975   "Homosexuals Focus for a Church," by James E. Adams, published.[76] (April 3)

1975   Third in a series of three articles is published, "Most Lesbians Live Quiety in World of Straights," and "Views Clash on Homosexual Causes," by Diane Stafford and David Zeeck.[77] (April 4)

1975   A panel discussion is conducted in the home of Mrs. Phyllis Shafer, mother of Drew Shafer, that included: Dr. Lofton Hudson, Staff Psychiatrist, *Midwest Christian Counseling Service*; Rev. Ronald D. Burcham; Mrs. Mary Beth B., Board of Director, *Metropolitan Community Church--Kansas City*; Mr. Joe Cecil, *Metropolitan Community Church--Kansas City*; and Mrs. Shafer, parent of a gay son and active member, *Metropolitan Community Church--Kansas City*.[78] (June 2)

1975   "Rights Groups Denounce Plan to Restrict Gay Bar Workers," by Robert L. Carroll, article published about Kansas City's liquor codes.[79] (October 23)

1970s (mid)   *K.C. Urban NOW* chapter started by Margit Lasker (she died of leukemia in 1977).[80]

1970s (mid)   Men's gay bars were began to allow lesbians entrance.[81]

1970s (mid)   *Midwest Women's Festival* began offering a week each year of "wimmin only" space in the Missouri woods.[82]

1976   *Gay Lib* sues University of Missouri. Federal Judge Elmo B. Hunter rules against *Gay Lib*.

1976   The Gay People's Union (GPU) ceased; Gay Community Services Center (GCSC) assumed the services of GPU, plus a crisis line.[83]

1976   *Liberation is for Everone* (LIFE) *Democratic Club* (LDC) was an independent club whose primary purpose was the investigation and endorsement of political candidates of all political parties, and the registration of voters in the gay and lesbian community. LDC lobbied within the Democratic Party and testified at the 1976 Democratic Party Platform Committee hearings. It even worked with a progressive Republican group.[84]

1976   The national spotlight falls on Kansas City's Kemper Arena, where the 1976 Republican National Convention is held. While Republicans were busy nominating Gerald Ford for president, members of the *National Coalition of Gay Activists* camped out with other event protesters at Penn Valley Park and passed out thousands of leaflets encouraging the repeal of sodomy laws.

1976   *Metropolitan Community Church of Kansas City* held its first sermon at their sanctuary at 4000 Harrison (purchased from First United Pentacostal Church and took possession on February 25), Rev. Ronald D. Burcham, officiating.[85] (February 29)

1976   *Heart of America Sunday Softball League* (HASSL)
            [originally just "Sunday Softball" and now (2011)
            "Heart of America Softball League"] was formed in
            Kansas City to provide a social outlet with a more
            athletic bent. The first game was in Waterworks
            Park in Turner, Kansas. Paul Rogers and Aggie
            Wheeler were the first two Board of Directors. In
            1980, they switched to a slow pitch league. And, in
            1983 HASSL joined a network of lesbian and gay
            softball leagues called the *North American Gay
            Amateur Athletics Alliance* (NAGAAA).[86] (Spring)

1976   "Real Facts Regarding Homosexuality,"
            published.[87] (August 16)

1976   Phyllis Shafer delivered a speech across the street
            opposite the entrance to U.S. President Gerald
            Ford's hotel headquarters at Crown Center. She
            also spent all evening (till 12:15 a.m.) at Kemper
            Arena outside where the Republican National
            Convention was held, demonstrating with gays
            representing the heterosexual mother of a gay son,
            helping fight for equal rights for homosexuals.
            Phyllis gave a short talk at random at Kemper.
            Mrs. Shafer's scrapbooks detail this event, and
            include gay literature passed out at the
            convention.[88] (August 17)

1976   "Gays Assert Right to Give out Leaflets," article by
            Lois Leuellyn published. Manfred Maier, attorney
            for the *National Coalition of Gay Activists*,
            mentioned in this article about the Republican
            National Convention.[89] (August 18)

1976   "Penn Valley Park Site of the Last of the
        Protestors," by Robert T. Nelson published. Also,
        "Yipee's 3-Ring Circus Rolling with Faith, Freaks
        and Frivolity," by Richard A. Serrano.[90]
        (August 19)

1976   "Gay Activists Take Protest to U. S. Prison in
        Leavenworth," article about allowing publications to
        be delivered in the U.S. Postal Service.[91] (August 20)

1976   "Gays March Out of the Closet in Support of
        Their Rights," by David L Langford. With
        homosexuals pouring out of the closet in ever-
        increasing numbers--including pro athletes,
        servicemen, clerics, and policemen--the gay rights
        movement is gaining momentum. Before the
        Republican National Con- vention in Kansas City,
        President Ford was asked during an appearance at
        Bradley University in Peoria to "clarify.
        Increasingly militant, gay liberationists are raising
        their voices for an end to repression of
        homosexuals.[92] (August 22)

1976   *Metropolitan Community Church of Kansas City*
        (MCC-KC) (As of 7 Sept 1993, *Spirit of Hope MCC*)
        dedication ceremonies for their location at 4000
        Harrison (purchased from First United Pentacostal
        Church). The first sermon at the Harrison location
        was February 29, 1976, Rev. Ronald D. Burcham
        officiating (he left the following month, in
        November 1976, for Australia).[93] (October 17)

1976   "Police Puzzled in Death of Man Found on
        Tracks," article about a man found in Kansas City,

Kansas, dressed partly in women's clothes.[94] (November 19)

1976   *Metropolitan Community Church of Kansas City* (MCC-KC) (As of 7 Sept 1993, *Spirit of Hope MCC*) welcomes Rev. Jim Glyer (from Los Angeles) as their new pastor; his first sermon was January 19, 1977.[95] (December)

1977   *Metropolitan Community Church of Kansas City* (MCC-KC) (As of 7 Sept 1993, *Spirit of Hope MCC*) launches a new couseling service by Keith Spare, Bob England and Barbara Price.[96]

1977   "Gays Across the U.S. Publicize Equal Rights Demands by Marching: Homosexuals React Against Anita Bryant." Article said about 30 showed up for a rally titled the 3rd annual *Heart of America Gay Pride Festival* in Kansas City.[97] (June 27)

1977   *The Christopher Street Association* (later *Christoper Street Project*) was formed to counter the Kansas City demonstration of fundamentalist Christian singer Anita Bryant's anti-gay "Save Our Children" campaign. Protesters picketed her venomous hate rally at Kansas City's Municipal Auditorium, and a candlelight march was planned; 500-600 protestors appeared against Bryant. Founders were: Lea Hopkins (Kansas City's first African-American Playboy bunny (and a lesbian) later moved onto the national scene); Judy Brock; Michael Tercey; Randy Stewart; and, Ken Hill (or Kenneth Green?), at the *Metropolitan Community Church-Kansas City (MCC-KC).*

Christopher Street Project was involved in other activities, including to strengthen the *Gay Student Union* (GSU) and the *Kansas University Gay and Lesbian Alliance* (KU-GALA). They provided material to local print and broadcast media and held workshops addressing racism. They worked with *Club Baths* to establish mobile VD testing, "VD Queen."

A patrol was established in Penn Valley Park at the Liberty Memorial when police began using harassment tactics against gays in the Park.

Christopher Street Project ceased in 1979.[98] (July 13)

1977   First *Gay and Lesbian Pride Parade* in Kansas City. (sponsored by *The Christopher Street Project*)[99]

1977	"Revelation: Homosexuals Cast Aside Mirage of Straight Life," by Michael Bauer published.[100] (July 24)

1977	"Gay Military is Strongest in U.S.," by Ray Smith published.[101] (August 6)

1977   *Willow Productions* was formed, offering 13 womens' music events a year. In the 1980s, two of

Willow Productions organizers moved to California to become Holly Near's producers. The entity's registration was forfeited by January 1985.[102] (August 12)

1977   Ann Landers continues to print that "homosexuality is a psychiatric disorder caused by one of several problems," despite the fact that the The American Psychiatric Association removes homosexuality from its Diagnostic and Statistical Manual of Mental Disorders in December 1973. Still, she advocated for "acceptance, understanding and compassion."[103] (September 8)

1977   *Gay Lib* appeals to the Eighth Circuit Court; wins 2-1 against University of Missouri to allow it to form on campus. The University petitions the Supreme Court on September 20 on grounds that the case against *Gay Lib* is a medical one. (September 20)

1977   *Metropolitan Community Church of Kansas City* (MCC-KC) (As of 7 Sept 1993, *Spirit of Hope MCC*) welcomed Rev. Rob Shivers (from MCC-Austin), as Assistant Pastor. She was the principal speaker at the 1974 Gay Pride Festival in Kansas City.[104] (October 1)

1977   "Supreme Court Ruling Against Gays," article published (October 4) about the Court denying certiorari (Justices Brennan and Marshall would have granted cert). This was the first homosexual discrimination decision to be aired on national network news. In fact, it was simultaneously aired on all three national network evening news shows, reaching approximately 60 million viewers.[105]

1977   **"Anita Bryant to Speak Hear," at Municipal Auditorium for her "Revive America Crusades" tour.**[106] **(October 10)**

1977   "Banana Crème Pie for Anita in Des Moines," airs on television when a gay activist shares some humble pie with homophobe Anita Bryant.[107] (October 14)

1977   **"Resolution Supports Gay Rights," by Helen T. Gray, publishes about the General Asembly of the Christian Church (Disciples of Christ) protesting civil liberties of homosexuals.**[108] **(October 24)**

1977   **"Gay Protest Moved to Columbia," article publishes.**[109] **(November 17)**

1977   "Consequences of a Crusade: Anita Bryant and the Gay Community," article publishes.[110] (November 20)

38

1978   *Gay Community Services Center* (GCSC) evolved into the *Gay Student Union* (GSU).[111]

1978   *Women's Liberation Union* (WLU) continued to narrow its focus, indentifying itself as socialist or feminist. Two off-shoots continued: *Actors Sorority* and the *Women's Chorus.*[112]

1978   Gay students at the University of Missouri filed a lawsuit against the University (in 1971) for their right to have the Gay People's Student Union be recognized with the same rights as other student groups on campus. The case (Ratchford, President, University of Missouri et al. vs. Gay Lib et al.) made it all the way to the Supreme Court, but the court refused to hear the case, thus upholding a previous court's decision and giving the gay student groups the right to assemble. The Supreme Court's non-decision strengthened the ability for gay campus groups to form at universities all over the United States. [113] (February 21)

1978   **Second Gay and Lesbian Pride Parade in Kansas City (sponsored by The Christopher Street Project). Rev. Troy D. Perry, founder of the MCC, guest speaker at All Souls Unitarian Church. 250 marchers for Gay Pride Week, June 16-24.[114] (June 17)**

1978   Steppin' Out Opens Doors, about The Club Baths chain of the 1970s and early 1980s, among the first of the baths to proudly print their name and insignia on matches, tee shirts, advertisements and other items. With locations in the USA from Akron to

Washington D.C. and abroad (including four locations in Canada), the Club Baths Chain was the largest gay bath house chain in the world, and one of the first openly gay businesses in North America.[115] (November 9)

1978   Slaying of San Francisco Supervisor, Harvey Milk, and San Franciso Mayor, George Moscone.[116] (November 27)

1979   First national homosexual rights march on the mall in Washington, DC, is held.[117]

1979   "Hot Stuff." "Bad Girls." "Dim All the Lights." *Bad Girls,* seventh studio album by disco (and gay) icon Donna Summer, releases on Casablanca Records. Originally issued as a double album, it incorporates musical styles of disco, soul, and rock. *Bad Girls* became the best-selling album of Summer's recording career, achieving double platinum sales certification in the United States, and selling approximately four million copies total worldwide. (April 25)

1979   **The Village People perform at Kemper Arena. (May 28)**

1979   **Third Gay and Lesbian Pride Parade in Kansas City (sponsored by *The Christopher Street Project.* 300 attendees.[118] (June 15)**

1979   ***Kansas City Gay Coalition, Inc.* founded.[119] (September 21)**

1979   **The *Christopher Street Project* ceased.**

1970s (late)   *The Joint Committee for Gay Rights* was organized to get a gay or lesbian representative appointed to Kansas City's Human Relations Department. Eventually, Rev. Jim Glyer, pastor at the *Metropolitan Community Church of Kansas City (MCC-KC)*, was appointed to the Commission. Glyer was succeeded by Keith Spare, who was an associate pastor at the church, and director of Gay Talk since it started in 1975. Gerry Young said, *"There were some great people on the commission who had come out for the gay issue. One young black man, Joseph Jones, a Republican, eventually got us a continuous seat on that commission."*[120]

1980   "Who's the Man Behind the Female Impersonator?" by Michael Bauer, article about Sandy Kay, with a photograph of Mickey Marlowe, Ronnie Summers and Bruce E. Winter (as Melinda Ryder).[121] (May 20)

Sandy Kay

1980   Fourth Gay and Lesbian Pride Parade in Kansas City.[122] (June)

1980   The Democratic National Convention becomes the first major political party in America to endorse a homosexual rights platform.[123]

1981	The first *Heart of America Softball Classic* softball tournament was put on by the *Kansas City Coed Sports Association* in Swope Park. Lesbian and gay teams from many cities came to Kansas City to compete. Later, the Classice was in Rosedale Park and between 1988 and 1991 it was in Cottonwood Park in Lenexa, Kansas.[124]
1981	The first five cases of mysterious disease is reported by the CDC in five homosexual men in Los Angeles. Initially, when the CDC began issuing warnings, the virus that eventually was named H.I.V. and the disease A.I.D.S. was called Gay Related Immuity Deficiency (G.R.I.D.) and/or HTLV-3.[125] (June 5)
1981	Fifth Gay and Lesbian Pride Parade in Kansas City.[126] (June)
1981	Associated Press story from Kansas City, "Special Groups Established: Gay Alcoholics Receive Help," publishes naming Bill Harvey who in 1979 established and listed in the phone book a gay referral service for "Gay alcoholics."[127] (May 18)
1981	The *Gay Organized Alliance for Liberation* (GOAL) began operation with the goals of public education and elimination of discrimination. One of their most significant accomplishments was a successful lawsuit against the Kansas City Area Tranportation Authority (KCATA), which had refused to place informational signs on its busses. With the legal support from the American Civil Liberties Union (ACLU) of Western Missouri and Kansas, GOAL was able to overturn this ban. In 1988, GOAL shifted its activities to educating the

lesbian and gay community. It ceased operations in 1989.[128] (July)

1981   *Gay and Lesbian News-Telegraph* (now just *News-Telegraph*), appeared as a monthly in St. Louis, Missouri. Early issues averaged 12 pages and they were distributed only in St. Louis. The current paper comes out twice a month and averages 44 pages. It has a distribution of 15000, two-thirds of it in the St. Louis and Kansas City metro areas, the rest in small towns through southern Illinois, Missouri, Kansas and northwest Arkansas.

General manager Jim Thomas says, "The idea behind starting the publication was to provide a solid base of information for gay and lesbian community development. In a sense, the mission was political. But to do it effectively, we felt it had to be an independent, objective newspaper of record. We accept that being gay and lesbian is a perfectly normal and acceptable thing. We are a paper of record for that community." Thomas denies that the paper has any unifying ideology. "We are as happy to run commentary pieces from people who identify themselves as conservatives as we are to run pieces by left-wing socialists who want to reach gay and lesbians."

The paper began as an all-volunteer, typewritten effort. Real growth started in 1990, after Thomas left his job at KWMU to work full-time on the News-Telegraph. The paper had to expand its territory, says Thomas, to support a paid staff and the production standards necessary to do quality journalism. It now has seven employees and two

43

offices. Additional gay publications now in St. Louis are TWISL and LesTalk. Thomas says they are not competitors, but have different functions, "One is a bar publication and the other is an advocacy magazine." KNLC, says director Larry Rice, went on the air in September 1983 with a multi-purpose approach:

To try to zero in on minorities, to promote local community programming, such as performances by central city choirs, "to be a voice for the indigent, the homeless and the elderly, the people who aren't normally heard" and to bring together people with resources and people with needs. From an article, "25 Years: The Ups and Downs of St. Louis Media," by Peter Downs.[129] (October 6)

1982   The term A.I.D.S. is first mentioned to identify/name the virus.

1982   Sixth Gay and Lesbian Pride Parade in Kansas City. [THERE WERE NO PRIDE PARADES IN 1983, 1984, 1985, 1986, 1987, AND 1988]; but, workshops and street fairs were held to celebrate Lesbian and Gay Pride Month in June, the anniversary of the Stonewall Riots].[130]

1982   Wisconsin becomes the first state legislature to outlaw discrimination on the basis of sexual orientation.[131]

1982   The first Gay Games takes place in San Francisco, drawing over 1,350 athletes.[132]

1982   *Metropolitan Community Church of Kansas City* (MCC-KC) (As of 7 Sept 1993, *Spirit of Hope MCC*) welcomed Rev. John Barbone, Pastor.[133] (May 2)

1982   The first report of A.I.D.S. being diagnosed in Kansas City reported to the *Kansas City Star* through the Kansas City Free Health Clinic. Gerry Young said, "At the close of the decade AIDS had claimed nearly 500 Kansas Citian's lives and between 10,000 and 15,000 were infected with HIV, 90% of them were gay men."[134] (October 14)

1983   Donald Gene Hayes, co-owner of "The Cabaret" and Morgan's Restaurant and Lounge at 208 Blue Ridge Boulevard, died. He was born in 1938, attended the First Baptist Church of Independence, and was buried in Mount Washinton Cemetery. He had been the Superintendent of the McCune Home for Boys in 1970.[135]

1983   Third *Heart of America Softball Classic* softball at 140th and Holmes.[136]

1983   *Gay Talk* organized as a 501(c)(3) not for profit corporation under the internal revenue service tax code.[137]

1983   There was NO Lesbian and Gay Pride Parade in Kansas City.[138] (June)

1983   "Gay America: Sex, Politics and the Impact of
            A.I.D.S." on the cover of Newsweek.[139] (August 8)

1984   A.I.D.S. is associated with H.I.V.[140]

1984   *Gay Services Network* (GSN) founded by Dennis
            Krell (4405 Harrison, K.C., MO); Eddie
            Edmondson (3809 Walnut Apt 1N, K.C., MO);
            and, Keith Spare (4515 Wyoming), with Cliff Dow
            (805 N Summit Cir, Blue Springs, MO); Ed Fink
            (5050 Oak, K.C., MO); and, Geoffrey H. Segebarth
            (3332 Baltimore Ave) as additional Board of
            Directors to provide the greater Kansas City area
            with a public telephone service for eduction,
            information, counseling and referrals. See May 21,
            1991, when GSN added "Lesbian" to its name.[141]
            (March 29)

1984   *Good Samaritan Project, Inc.*, founded in Kansas
            City as a not-for-profit A.I.D.S. service
            organization. Previously, it had been called *Heart
            of America Human Services, Inc.*; and originally,
            *Gay/Lesbian Health Clinic of Greater Kansas City,
            Inc.* The original incorporators were: Wayne
            Arndt, 1705 S. Kiger, Independence, Missouri; Joe
            Schommer, 114 W. 34th Street, Kansas City,
            Missouri; Eddie Leidtke, 3828 Wyandotte Apt. 1N,
            Kansas City, Missouri; and, Steven K. Bolger, 818
            Grand Ave Ste 700, Kansas City, Missouri.

            Begun by volunteers who gathered in the basement
            of the *Metropolitan Community Church*, *Good
            Samaritan Project* is Kansas City's oldest and most
            comprehensive agency exclusively devoted to the
            care and prevention of H.I.V./A.I.D.S. They

opened the "Good Samaritan House" at an undisclosed location in Midtown Kansas City--to protect its residents from hate crimes. They helped with peer counseling, transportation, food and clothing. Initially, the home served 5-6 men. The Project's *Good Samaritan House* closed in 1988. The agency in 2010 maintains a staff of more than 20 professionals and over 100 volunteers. The service area consists of 11-counties in greater Kansas City. GSP offices are located in Kansas City, Missouri, and in Kansas City, Kansas.[142] (May 1)

Gary Root said, *"Everybody was involved with everybody to take care of the people with AIDS. There were hundreds of volunteers. It was all very awful then. Drugs had to be shipped around incognito for people dying that didn't have insurance. They couldn't stay in the hospitals and the nursing homes wouldn't accept them. People would sometimes come in the morning and die later in the evening. It was like when you're old and all of your friends are dying except everybody was really young. Social events were fundraisers and funerals."[143]*

1984   *Kansas City Gay Pride, Inc.* founded. Steven K. Bolger (818 Grand Ave Ste 700, K.C., MO) was a registered agent.[144] (May 11)

1984   There was NO Lesbian and Gay Pride Parade in Kansas City.[145] (June)

1984   "A.I.D.S. Still Taking Lives in Kansas City area," article by Lisa Massoth published about the death of Dennis Krell.[146] (August 14)

1984   "Coming Out Together," article discusses how both politics and religion play an important role in the search by Kansas City's gay community for a voice, a face and share of power. Article by Eden Stone.[147] (August)

1985   There was NO Lesbian and Gay Pride Parade in Kansas City.[148] (June)

1985   A spokesperson for actor Rock Hudson acknowledges the star has A.I.D.S., bringing the disease to the media forefront for the first time. Hudson (born Roy Harold Scherer, Jr. and changed later Roy Harold Fitzgerald) died on October 2.[149] (July 25)

1986   *Oklahoma Gay Rodeo Association* combines efforts with *Kansas and Missouri Gay Rodeo Associations* to host first *Great Plains Regional Rodeo*.

1986   The genesis of *PROMO* is founded in St. Louis as the Privacy Rights Education Project (PREP). In June 2004, Greg Razer served as Field Organizer for PROMO's Western Missouri office. PROMO is Missouri's only statewide LGBT human rights organization. But, when it was PREP, it first started totally as a privacy rights organization for LGBT, women's rights, people with H.I.V./A.I.D.S., and so on. Razer points out that, "it morphed into a LGBT civil rights organization," Around 2000 they changed their name to PROMO." Probably PROMO's biggest success story was in 1999, when they successfully lobbied to have Missouri's Hate Crimes Bill-including sexual orientation--passed. Missouri was the only state in the union to have a Hate Crimes

Bill passed that year; the same year as Matthew Shepard's murder. "And we are still one of the few states whose Hate Crimes Bill includes gender identity." Razer proudly proclaims.[150]

1986   *Heartland Men's Chorus* (HMC) founded. The first HMC concert was at Pierson Hall at the University of Missouri--Kansas City. The members of HMC have joined together for the purpose of making music as a not-for-profit, volunteer chorus of gay and gay-sensitive people who are making a positive cultural contribution to the entire community. They are a member of GALA Choruses, the international association of the lesbian and gay choral movement. Founded in 1982, GALA Choruses represents 190 choruses, their 10,000 singers and 750,000 patrons in Australia, Europe, South America, and North America. The HMC has donated and begun transferring historical materials to the Gay and Lesbian Archive of Mid-America (GLAMA).[151]

1986   There was NO Lesbian and Gay Pride Parade in Kansas City.[152] (June)

1986   *Lesbian Convention* (sponsored by "*Talking Dykes*"). The idea for the *Lavender Umbrella*—Kansas City's first Lesbian Center—was conceived (see March 1987).[153] (June 9)

1986   *S.A.V.E. Foundation, Inc.* [SAVE, Inc.] founded in Kansas City by Father Richard F. Carney; Dan D. Zimmerman, M.D.; and, Neal Colby, Jr. The group of altruistic volunteers recognized the dire

need for housing for those dying from
H.I.V./A.I.D.S.[154]
(August 12)

1986   "*Lavender Umbrella* as an organization has existed
for more than six months and sponsored two
events including the Susan B. Anthony Dance at
the YWCA." *Lavender Umbrella* is a membership
organization and use the monthly membership
pledges to pay the expenses of rent, utilities, phone
and events. Monthly pledges are on a sliding scale.
Every member receives her own Lavender I.D.
declaring her an, "official card carrying lesbian."[155]
(September)

1987   While the Federal government remained silent on
the issue of A.I.D.S., Kansas City Mayor, Dick
Berkeley, appointed the City's leading local
philanthropist, Marian Kramer, to form the
A.I.D.S. Council.[156]

1987   AZT approved as the drug to treat patients with
H.I.V. and A.I.D.S. It was about the only drug for
many years. It had to be taken EVERY 4 HOURS
around the clock.[157]

1987   *Pink Triangle Political Coalition* (PTPC) organizes
as a result of the National March on Washington
for Lesbian and Gay rights. PTPC member Joe
Kent was selected as a delegate to the Kansas
Democratic Convention where she addressed
conference delegates.[158]

1987   When A.I.D.S. becomes a concern to the gay
community, *Gay Talk* volunteers began a speaker's

bureau, which offered lectures and workshops on H.I.V. and A.I.D.S. These services were in such high demand that a separate program, *Condom Crusaders*, was created in 1987. *Condom Crusaders*, through 2001, provided safer-sex packet distribution at Kansas City public-sex areas and Kansas City's gay and lesbian bars.

1987   *Gay Talk* restructures the organization as an umbrella not-for-profit, expands the organization's mission statement and changes the official name to *Gay Services Network, Inc.* (GSN) This allowed for many new programs to be created without applying for separate not for profit status for each program.

1987   Kansas City's first lesbian center becomes a reality (see March 1986). *Lavender Umbrella* is a storefront at 306-08 East 43rd Street with meeting spaces, an office and a small courtyard. It has been planned as a gathering place for lesbians and their women friends.[159] (March 20)

1987   U.S. President Ronald Reagan first mentions A.I.D.S., after 20,849 of his own citizens had died from it.[160] (May)

1987   There was NO Lesbian and Gay Pride Parade in Kansas City.[161] (June)

1987   National March on Washington for Lesbian and Gay Rights and the *Names' Project A.I.D.S. Quilt.*[162] (October 23)

1988   *The Good Samaritan Project* closes "Good Samaritan House."[163]

1988   *S.A.V.E. Foundation, Inc.* [SAVE, Inc.] secures a $100,000 grant from the Missouri state government to establish SAVE Home, the first 24-hour hospice in the state of Missouri specifically for A.I.D.S. patients. From this humble act, SAVE has since grown into the leading social service housing agency in Kansas City for those living with or at risk for H.I.V./A.I.D.S., helping nearly 700 individuals and families every single month find safe, stable, and affordable place to call home. SAVE, Inc. services a 15-county radius and offers assisted living, referral services, rent and utility assistance, emergency assistance funds, and transitional and permanent housing.

1988   There was NO Lesbian and Gay Pride Parade in Kansas City. However, the first A.*I.D.S. Walk* (originally called, "*Walk for Life*") sponsored by *SAVE, Inc.*, took place in Theiss Park between 47th Street (today Cleaver Boulevard, II) on the south side of the Nelson-Atkins Museum of Art and Volker Boulevard.

Steve Metzler said, *"Not the first year, but the second year...in those days we walked what seemed like forever because we used to do pledges in those days by-the-mile, so we walked all the way to Waldo. Whose idea was this? So we shortened it."* A.I.D.S. Walk T-Shirts for each year were preserved by Terry Newell and Mike Sugnet, to keep the memory of all the people Kansas City lost over all the years to A.I.D.S. so that we never lose sight of why we are out there and what we are there for. This collection was donated to the Gay and Lesbian Archive of Mid-America (GLAMA) in 2009.[164] (June)

1988   *Evoke* was created by the *Gay Services Network* (GSN) to provide gay and lesbian awareness training to the Kansas City Police Department from 1988 to 1994. In 1994 the KCPD incorporated Evoke's training materials into their standard officer training courses.

1989   *The Tenth Voice* radio program piloted on KKFI.[165] (January)

1989   Larry Gilbert opens, "Larry's Cards and Gifts." (See New Earth Books and Phoenix bookstore entries.) He sold in August 2002 to "In the Life;" but, returned when they foundered in September 2004 to open again as, "OutThere."[166]

1989   Sheila Kemper Deitrich contacted Steve Metzler, then with S.A.V.E. Foundation, Inc. [SAVE, Inc.], who had been approached by Sandy Berkeley. Composer, Christopher Lacy, and a group from St. Paul's Episcopal Church at 40th and Main in Kansas City, had composed a Requiem Project. Mrs. Dietrich and Mrs. Berkeley took extraordinary risks and led the charge to stage a fundraiser for *SAVE Home*. This was the first major A.I.D.S. fundraiser in Kansas City.

They asked the Kansas City Symphony to donate their time to play an unheard Requiem. A number of soloists donated their time and talents to SAVE. Barkeley and Evergreen created the invitations. University Club (now Kansas City Club) provided the after-party. The event turned out the A-list of Kansas City. It raised over $100,000 for SAVE, Inc. Steve Metzler said, "*All the flowers were donated. But, what wasn't clearly communicated was that the flowers used for the event were going to be re-purposed for weddings and other events the following weekend.... [We rushed around town to find where they had gone to return as many as we could to a variety of florists who needed them for other events.]*"[167] (May 25)

1989   Second annual A.I.D.S. Walk

1989   Drew Shafer died of A.I.D.S., twenty-one years and twenty-nine days after his twenty-first anniversary with Mickey Ray. Shafer was unarguably one of the leading proponents of the "gay liberation" movement in Kansas City.[168] (September 30)

1990   Third annual A.I.D.S. Walk. (April)

1990   *Greater Kansas City Gay and Lesbian Youth Services, Inc.*, began an association of mental health professionals and interested volunteers to provide support and educational services for lesbian, gay, bisexual, transgender, and questioning (LGBTQ) youth confronting questions of sexual identity and homophobia. The group later changed their name to "Passages." Passages is Kansas City's only youth program dedicated to gay, lesbian, bisexual, transgender, and questioning youth. Passages helps encourage youth to grow and develop in a drug-free, alcohol-free, and hate-free environment, and to continue to support them as they discover who they are, no matter what their orientation or gender. Thousands of youth have passed through their doors over the years. [See 1994 and December 2003, 2004 and 2008 entries for transitions.][169] (August 8)

1990   An effort to ammend Kansas City's civil rights law to include sexual orientation failed.[170]

1990s (early)   *Cultural Exchange* was formed in Kansas City.[171]

1990s (early) *Rainbow Awards Committee* was formed in Kansas City.[172]

1991 *The Corporation of Gay and Lesbian Awareness/Gay Pride of Greater Kansas City* (GALA) (with Bill Todd as President) merged with *Gay Services Network* (GSN) (with Steven R. Pierce as President) merged. GSN was the surviving corporation. GALA was thereinafter a division of GSN.[173] (January 1)

1991 *Lesbians for Justice* formed.[174]

1991 From 1991 to 2000, *Gay and Lesbian Services Network, Inc.* was the lead training agency for the City of Kansas City, MO Health Department H.I.V. Health Education/Risk Reduction Program. GLSN provided training to other non-profit agencies that received HE/RR grant funding.

1991 *Gay Services Network, Inc.*, (GSN) added 'and Lesbian' to its name, creating the present *Gay and Lesbian Services Network, Inc.* (located at 9813 Drury Ave, K.C., MO). "Since 1987, GLSN has provided a 'home' for many single-goal organizations such as: Gay and Lesbian Awareness: created to host various gay and lesbian oriented entertainment events from 1987 to 1992." [According to the charter filed with the Missouri Secretary of State, GSN has been operating since 1984.][175] (May 21)

1991 Fourth annual A.I.D.S. Walk. (April)

1991 "Callers urge Cleaver to spurn gay pride week: City Hall lines tied up by those opposed to recognition of the event," article by Mary Sanchez, Staff Writer, published. City Hall telephone lines have been clogged by up to 700 callers a day who hope to keep Kansas City Mayor Emanuel Cleaver from formally recognizing the 1991 Gay and Lesbian Pride Week. Pride organizers asked Cleaver to issue a proclamation in honor of the week's activities, which are scheduled to begin Saturday. But two local Christian radio stations publicized the request, prompting the phone calls to City Hall.[176] (June 14)

1992 *The Lesbian and Gay Community Center of Kansas City* (LGCC-KC) founded. The Center is an open, public and visible safe space for individuals and organizations in the LGBT and allied community, providing referral services and information, networking opportunities and access to other LGBT-supportive groups and businesses.[177]

1992 11th annual *Heart of America Softball Classic* softball at 140th and Holmes.[178] (March)

1992 "Council votes to support Gay, Lesbian Pride Week," article by James C. Fitzpatrick and Mary Sanchez, Staff Writers published. The City of Kansas City becomes the second area municipality to officially recognize June 12-21 as Gay and Lesbian Pride Week. On an 8-0 vote, the City Council adopted a resolution designating the week and commending the gay and lesbian community for raising awareness of "the unique problems and challenges"facing gay men and lesbian women."[179] (May 16)

1992   Fifth annual A.I.D.S. Walk (April)

1992   Kansas City City Council sets up a *Human Rights Commission.*[180] (August)

1992   *A.I.D.S. Service Foundation of Greater Kansas City* founded by Sandra L. "Sandy" Schermerhorn, then Board President of the Good Samaritan Project, and Kansas City dentist Dave (Forber?). He left and went to New Mexico after six months, and Steve Metzler took his place as President of A.I.D.S. Service Foundation) led volunteers from four organizations to work to raise money and awareness for organizations that provide shelter, medical care and emergency services for the more men, women and children in Kansas City affected by H.I.V./A.I.D.S.

Incorporation papers reveal the Foundation was originally designed to raise funds for four organizations: 1) the Good Samaritan Project, 2) Heartland A.I.D.S. Resource Council (food pantry), 3) Kansas City Free Health Clinic, and 4) SAVE, Inc. Each organization originally committed to contribute $5,000 to the Foundation. Each organization would have two representatives on the Board for a total of eight, and they would appoint members of the community at large for diversity. They also devised a funding formula that would also provide funding to the community (and the "Community Fund" was born).

As of 2010, contributions to the A.I.D.S. Service
Foundation benefit equally 1) the Kansas City Free
Health Clinic; 2) SAVE, Inc.; 3) Good Samaritan
Project; 4) Hope Care Center; and, 5) the A.I.D.S.
Service Foundation Community Fund. The
A.I.D.S. Service Foundation "Community Fund"
awards grants to not-for-profit organizations that
service the specialized needs of the diverse
communities dealing with H.I.V./A.I.D.S., provide
support to their families and friends, and/or
promote education and prevention. Other
programs include: "Arts Audiences Against
A.I.D.S.;" "A.I.D.S. Walk;" "Ribbon of Hope
Awards Dinner (started in 1993 and lasted for a
decade);" and "Coterie Theater's Dramatic A.I.D.S.
Education Project," in conjuction with the Kansas
University Medical Center, where volunteer
doctors and actors go into schools and talk about
A.I.D.S.[181] (August 25)

1992   Mary Fisher, founder, Family A.I.D.S. Network,
            spoke at the Republican National Convention in
            Houston, Texas. A risk taker, she said she was,
            "white, rich, woman, Jewish, blonde, and H.I.V.
            positive."[182]

1992   "A matter of citizenship." The issue of homosexuals
            in the military is a hot subject that needs a cool
            approach. This article discusses President Clinton's
            answer to the subject. See also, "The Compromise,"
            on 21 July 1993.[183] (November 11)

1992   *A.I.D.S. Service Foundation of Greater Kansas City's*
            first fundraiser was a "Sock Hop" at the Municipal

Auditorium. A snowstorm and other mishaps, the event lost $15,000. (December)

1992   "Revised Gay Rights Code More than 'Routine' Now," article by Tim O'Neil (Ellen Futterman of the St. Louis Post-Dispatch staff contributed information for this story) published. A civil rights protection for homosexuals that is causing a fuss in Kansas City was adopted quietly in St. Louis two months ago. The St. Louis Board of Aldermen voted 28-0 without debate to approve a revised civil rights code that bans discrimination based upon ""sexual orientation,"" along with race, religion, sex and other factors. Mayor Vincent C. Schoemehl, Jr., signed it into law Oct. 16. The Kansas City Council set up a *Human Rights Commission* in August...."[184] (December 13)

1993   *A.I.D.S. Service Foundation of Greater Kansas City's* first "Ribbon of Hope Awards Dinner." Carol Swanson Price, wife of Ambassador Charles Price, and Adelle Hall worked as honorary chairs. Mary Fisher was invited as the first speaker. Fred Phelps showed up and picketed across the street. Other speakers in years following were: Mr. and Mrs. Dude Angus, member of the International Rotary Club who lost his son to A.I.D.S.; Judith Billings, H.I.V. positive from a sperm donation. The "Ribbon of Awards Hope" dinner raised over $10 million in the 10 years that it was offered before discontinuing in 2003.[185]

1993   The "Don't Ask, Don't Tell" policy is instituted for the U.S. military, permitting gays to serve in the military but banning activity. Thousands of gay and lesbian persons are relieved of their positions. See September 11, 2011.[186] (December 21)

1993   *Project Pride* created by *Gay and Lesbian Services Network* to host the 1993 to 1996 Kansas City Gay Pride Festivals.

1993   "A parallel in past," article by Kelly Garbus. When President Truman desegregated the military in 1948, he challenged stereotypes and enraged the South. His executive order now is considered a civil rights breakthrough. That kind of confrontation echoes today. President Clinton's proposal to end a ban on homosexual behavior in the military has split the country and put civil rights on a collision course with traditional moral standards. When Truman integrated the armed forces with Executive Order No. 9981....[187] (February 6)

1993   "Leading lives of quiet isolation Gay people say they must endure fear and loneliness in small towns," article by, Scott Canon, Mid-America Correspondent, published. To be gay in a small town means plenty of driving. It can mean drives of hundreds of miles, often to gay bars and neighborhoods of bigger cities. The attraction is to talk with like-minded people as much as it is to have sex with them. And then they drive home. Most often, alone. Gay men and women in rural Kansas and Missouri talk of an isolation that runs through everything they do."[188] (February 7)

1993   *The Official Miss Gay Kansas City America Pageant* chartered by Bruce E. Winter and R. Kirk Nelson (both at 520 W 12th Ste 304, Kansas City, Missouri). Winter and Nelson have donated selected performance apparel to the Gay and Lesbian Archive of Mid-Ame (April 5)

Bruce E. Winter as Melinda Ryder

1993   "Gay, lesbian marchers anticipate historic weekend: Many from K.C. join the march on Washington," article by Mary Sanchez published. More than a thousand people from the Kansas City area are expected to travel to Washington this weekend for what is being billed as the largest civil rights demonstration in U.S. history. Organizers of the 1993 March On Washington For Lesbian, Gay And Bi Equal Rights and Liberation expect more than a million people to create a procession Sunday in the mall area near the White House."[190] (April 23)

1993   Sixth annual A.I.D.S. Walk (April)

1993	"The Compromise," article by E. Thomas McClanahan reports on the " Don't Ask, Don't Tell" policy.[191] (July 21)
1993	*Metropolitan Community Church of Kansas City* (MCC-KC) became *Spirit of Hope MCC.*[192] (September 7)
1994	The City of Kansas City passed the Civil Rights Ordinance creating in its current form the Human Rights Commission.[193]
1994	*Gay Games-K.C.* created by *Gay and Lesbian Services Network* to represent Kansas City at the International Gay Games in New York, NY.
1994	Gay and Lesbian Pride Festival (sponsored by Project Pride)
1994	*Passages Youth Group* (previously created by *Gay and Lesbian Services Network* (GLSN) to provide a safe, non-threatening environment for teenage and young adult gays and lesbians) is transferred to the umbrella not-for-profit *Westport Cooperative Services, Inc.* By moving the program to WCS, Passages was able to expand its range of services and outreach efforts.
1994?	*Missouri on the Move* created by *Gay and Lesbian Services Network* to provide non-political educational services for Missouri on the Forefront in their effort to defeat the Missouri Constitutional Amendment that would have forbidden any laws or regulations that would

protect the rights of gay and lesbian citizens of Missouri.

1994   "Gay role quieter in KCs past," and "Many build fences between workplace, private lives," full-page article by Scott Cannon published, discussing what it was like to live in Kansas City in the 1950s [when police *"just seemed to lose interest...they decide to leave the (gay) bars aline, figuring that if the bars were going at least they'd know where everybody was."* There were also *"these guys who had these great big picnics in North Kansas City every year* (in the 50s and 60s). *They'd have a 'pasture party...' and a couple hundred gay people would show up."*], the 1960s [when *"hundreds flocked to the annual gay ball, held at the Muehlebach Hotel one year, the State Hotel in Kansas City, Kansas, the next. It remained on the move because no hotel would allow a repeat performance after watching so many men in drag stroll through its lobby."*], and the 1970s [when the *"local gay crowd had its own service organization, the Ten Four Hundred Club, named for the address of one of its members."*][194] (March 20)

1994   Seventh annual A.I.D.S. Walk (April)

1994   Missie B's opens as a piano lounge. Belle Starr began doing Monday night drag shows not knowing that they would soon be known for thier drag shows. They are currently (2010) the number one Drag Bar in Kansas City featuring the best in female impersonation and have shows 5 nights a week. In addition, they offer karoke two nights a week.[195] (April)

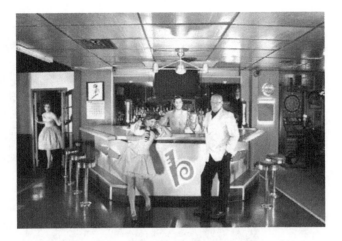

Ingenious homepage of missiebs.com

1994   *CAMP magazine* started by John Long and Jim Gabel at the Gay Pride Festival in Kansas City. ""MidWest Times", which was similar in content, had folded, and we felt there was a need for a publication that offered affordable advertising for small businesses and nonprofit groups and that served as a resource for the LGBT community. It helped knowing other writers from "MidWest Times" who might come on board to help us launch Camp. Two of these original writers, Bradley Osborn and Paul Donovan, are still providing their wonderful stories to us even now."

CAMP has donated their non-current, historical collection to the Gay and Lesbian Archive of Mid-America (GLAMA).[196] (June)

Kansas City Mayor, Kay Barnes, photographer, Dusti Cunningham, and stylist, Andy Chambers. "Dusti and Andy conceived the entire Kay Barnes Camp cover shoot, including picking out her outfit, wig, jewelry and the rainbow cake," said John Long. She was a real trooper, and Barnes said, "I _was_ June Cleaver." John added, "Dusti and Andy worked as a team for years and have done some of Camp's most creative covers."

1994   "Gay activism preceded fight at Stonewall: KC had homosexual rights movement before the violent raid on New York bar," article by Mary Sanchez, staff writer, published. The passage of time affects history; memories wither, photos deteriorate, records are lost - all of which allow the opportunity to polish an image and amplify its significance. Such is the fate of the Stonewall Inn and what happened there during several riotous nights beginning in the early morning hours of June 28, 1969. The events at Stonewall, a bar in New York's Greenwich Village, are commonly referred to as the beginning of the gay rights movement. This article reveals perspectives from Scoop Phillips that "from 1967 through the early 1970s, "*The Ladder,*" a national gay newsletter, was edited from Kansas City.... And that same year, The Phoenix Society opened the first local homosexual community center near Linwood Boulevard and The Paseo."[197] (June 27)

1994   Tim Van Zandt, a Democrat, elected as the first openly gay member ever elected to the Missouri General Assembly. He served eight years (through 2002) in the Missouri House of Representatives representing Kansas City. In a reliably Democratic district, he won the primary election held on August 2, 1994 with over 80% of the vote. He then faced only a Libertarian opponent in the general election, winning easily and taking office the following January. He was subsequently re-elected in 1996, 1998, and in 2000. Term limits prevented him from seeking re-election in 2002.[198] (August 2)

1995   *Lesbian and Gay Community Center of Greater Kansas City* is charted by Kevin Chafin (6120 Charlotte, K.C., MO); Elizabeth Massey (6109 W 54th St. Terr, Shawnee Mission, KS); and Lois Reborne (5806 Charlotte, K.C., MO).[199] (March 2)

1995   Eigth annual A.I.D.S. Walk (April)

1995   Gay and Lesbian Pride Festival (sponsored by Project Pride)

1996   Ninth annual A.I.D.S. Walk (April)

1996   Gay and Lesbian Pride Festival (sponsored by Project Pride)

1996   The Supreme Court strikes down Colorado's Amendment 2, which denied gays and lesbians protections against discrimination.[200]

1997   Ron Megee and Company's Late Night Theatre's production of "The Birds," a scandalous, funny, and irreverent satire of Hitchcock's horror film, staged at the former Old Chelsea strip club in the River Market, put the troop on the map ("although they had been around for several years,

putting on shows where they could find space,
whether in somebody's apartment living room or
during unused times at the Unicorn Theatre.")[201]

1997   Tenth annual A.I.D.S. Walk (April)

1997   Ellen Degeneres' character, Ellen Morgan, comes out
              as a lesbian on the popular sit-com, "Ellen," drawing
              36 million viewers. Did you host or attend a house
              party to watch the historic eipsode?[202]

1997   *National Institute for Gay, Lesbian, Bisexual and
              Transgender Education* founded (formerly the
              Norman Institute for Gay and Lesbian Studies, Inc.)
              by Dr. Terry L. Norman (330 W 47th Ste 212,
              Kansas City, Missouri); Ann Reskovak (3739
              Gillham, Kansas City, Missouri); Megan Monroe
              (2909 W 49th Terr, Westwood, Kansas); Jeanne
              Korman (4532 Jefferson Apt 3, Kansas City,
              Missouri); Mark Sappington (5302 Cherry, Kanas
              City, Missouri); and Chris Engman (330 W 47th St,
              Kansas City, Missouri) to dissemenate factual
              information about issues concerning gender
              orientation. General information about this now

defunct organization, and its groundbreaking online magazine, authenticity.org, edited by David W. Jackson, have been donated to the Gay and Lesbian Archive of Mid-America (GLAMA). (October 14)

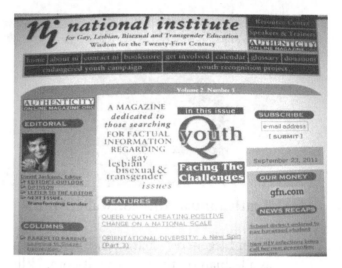

1998   *Parents, Families and Friends of Lesbians and Gays, Greater Kansas City Chapter, Inc.* (PFLAG) founded by Thomas C. Guyot (3611 Main #107-204, Kansas City, Missouri) and Mrs. Helen Cohen as registered agent (716 W Red Bridge Rd, Kansas City, Missouri).[203] (January 20)

1998   "Gay, lesbian couples will protest ban on same-sex marriages in Kansas City," article by Mary Sanchez published. "Valentine's Day and marriage would seem perfect companions. But gay and lesbian couples cannot legally marry in the United States. So for many such couples, this week is the perfect time to protest that barrier. In Kansas City and cities around the nation, demonstrations are planned for today, which has been dubbed National Freedom to Marry Day...."[204] (February 12)

1998   "GLAAD Calls Kansas City Home," article discusses the opening of a national office of the *Gay and Lesbian Alliance Against Defamation* (GLAAD), a media watchdog group.[205] (March 5-11)

1998   Eleventh annual A.I.D.S. Walk (April)

1998   Gays and lesbians show their pride in a parade (the first parade in morth than a decade) in Pridefest '98. Among the festivities are entertainers and 50 exhibit booths. The parade had about 100 entries from businesses,  organizations and groups in the gay and lesbian community.[206] (June 7)

1998   "Christianity and Homosexuality Coexist at Two Northland Churches," article published.[207] (July 9-15, 1998)

1998   Four Freedoms Democratic Club chartered. Megan J. Cramer, 4051 Broadway, Ste 103, Kansas City,

Missouri, 64111, is the registered agent.[208] (August 31)

1998   Matthew Shepard, a 21-year-old student at the University of Wyoming, was tortured and murdered near Laramie, Wyoming. He was attacked on the night of October 6–7, and died at Poudre Valley Hospital in Fort Collins, Colorado, on October 12 from severe head injuries.[209] (October 12)

1999   **Tivoli Cinemas kicks of its first "Kansas City Gay and Lesbian Film and Video Festival."[210]**

1999   **The Kansas City Women's Chorus, a non-profit, community based choral group forms to create a positive musical contribution to the community.[211]**

1999   **Twelfth annual A.I.D.S. Walk (April)**

1999   **"Gay Prom Offers Shelter from Discrimination," article describes the first gay prom held in the Kansas City area, sponsored by Passages, a gay and lesbian youth organization.[212] (June 24-30)**

1999   **"Finding a Place to Just Fit In," article dissuses the efforts of gay university staff and students to enact non-discriminatory practices on the campuses of Kansas City-area universities.[213] (August)**

2000   **PREP (see 1984) changed its name to PROMO.[214]**

2000   Vermont becomes the first state in the country to legally recognize civil unions between gay or lesbian couples.[215]

2000	The number of *Gay Talk* calls to the hotline had dropped dramatically. *Gay Talk* volunteers decided to transform *Gay Talk* into a web-based information center and discontinued the telephone hotline.[216] (January)
2000	"Outing the Census," article discusses how the 2000 Census allows for a count of "unmarried partners," and described one gay couple's marriage ceremony.[217] (April 20-26)
2000	Thirteenth annual A.I.D.S. Walk (April)
2000	"Pink-Triangle Dancing," article discusses the activities of the *Sho-Me Squares*, a gay square dancing club.[218] (July 27-Aug 2)
2000	"Gay Studies," article discusses the activities of the *Gay, Lesbian, Straight Education Network* in Kansas City area high schools.[219] (October 12-18)
2001	A.I.D.S. and Gay Catholic Priests. On Jan 30, 2001, *The Kansas City Star* launches the first of a three-day series of articles written by staff writer, Judy Thomas, about Catholic Priests dying of A.I.D.S. The front-page series, which sparked national media attention, dealt with many issues surrounding the A.I.D.S.-related deaths of Catholic priests, including the implication that many of the infected priests acquired the disease through homosexual relations.[220] (January 20)
2001	Fourteenth annual A.I.D.S. Walk (April)

2002   *Midwest Alternative Family Alliance* organizes by a
small group of people in Kansas City concerned
that local gay and lesbian parents and prospective
parents needed a presence, a voice, and a way to
connect with each other. In 2005, MAFA became a
501c3 non-profit organization. MAFA supports
LGBT parents in the greater Kansas City area and
beyond to build families and raise children in a
community that is respectful, encouraging, and
inclusive.[221]

2002   Fifteenth annual A.I.D.S. Walk (April)

2003   The last "Ribbon of Hope Awards Dinner,"
fundraiser of the *A.I.D.S. Service Foundation of
Greater Kansas City*. The organization then helped
to form "World A.I.D.S. Day," to try and prevent
complacency from setting in, and keeping people
engaged.[222]

2003   The City of Kansas City considers employee
benefits for gay, lesbian and unmarried couples.[223]
(April 24)

2003   Sixteenth annual A.I.D.S. Walk (April)

2003   *Kansas City Anti-Violence Project* founded to end
all types of violence in the lives of lesbian, gay,
bisexual, and transgender people. Part support,
and part education, KCAVP works toward a vision
of ending "all types of violence in the lives of
lesbian, gay, bisexual, and transgender (LGBT)
people." To that end, KCAVP provides: court
advocacy, emergency assistance, training sessions,

community organizing, statistical reporting, as well as other forms of help and outreach.[224] (June)

2003   The Lesbian, Gay, Bisexual, Transgender (LGBT) Office is launched out of the Women's Center as the LGBT Initiative in order to establish a physical presence for lesbian, gay, bisexual, and transgender individuals at the University of Missouri—Kansas City. A break-through project of the UMKC. Diversity in Action Plan (Project 6), the mission of the LGBT Office is to celebrate and honor the culture, history and accomplishments of lesbian, gay, bisexual, and transgender people. Today the office has grown to include QIA (Queer, Intersex and Ally) in our name. Most often the office will be noted as LGBTQIA Programs and Services. While it may seem cumbersome at first, the addition of QIA will allow us to be more inclusive in achieving our mission. UMKC. is one of 90 + universities in the United States with a professionally staffed LGBTQIA office or center.[225]

2003   *Show Me Pride, LLC*, founded for entertainment and productions by Melvin G. McMurtey and Rebecca R. Darnell. Show Me Pride announced Pride Week (June 1-6, 2010) culminating with the 32nd Pride Festival on Saturday, June 5, and Sunday, June 6. On these days, over 30,000 people from the midwest came together for one of the most exciting festivals of the year.[226] (July 3)

2003   Gay community celebrates 'genuinely joyous' day affirming gay rights in historic Supreme Court ruling striking down a Texas law (Lawrence v.

Texas) that laws prohibiting sodomy are
unconstitutional.[227]
(July 27)

2003   *Greater Kansas City Gay and Lesbian Chamber of
Commerce* founded.[228] (August 13)

2003   *Passages* unified with the *Lesbian and Gay
Community Center of Kansas City.* (December)

2004   Passages Youth Center moves to a new space

2004   A.I.D.S. Service Foundation hosts the first (of
what becomes an annual) A.I.D.S. bicycle
challenge.

2004   Seventeenth annual A.I.D.S. Walk (April)

2004   Same-sex marriages becomes legal in Massachusetts.[229]
(May 17)

2004	Missouri voters amend the State Constitution to ban marriage for gays and lesbians.[230] (August)
2005	Eigteenth annual A.I.D.S. Walk (April)
2005	Civil unions become legal in Connecticut.[231] (October)
2005	The Lesbian, Gay, Bisexual, Transgender (LGBT) Office at University of Missouri-Kansas City (UMKC.) held a tour of Kansas City's LGBT history, guided by Dr. Thomas Poe, chair of the Department of Communication Studies.[232]
2006	Missouri removes sodomy laws from its books (which had been there sine 1812 when Missouri became a territory).
2006	The LGBT Office at University of Missouri-Kansas City holds a second tour of Kansas City's LGBT history, guided by Dr. Thomas Poe, chair of the Department of Communication Studies.[233]
2006	Nineteenth annual A.I.D.S. Walk (April)
2006	"Our Community's Radio Show: The Tenth Voice," article by Bradley Osborn profiling the producers and hosts of "The Tenth Voice," a weekly radio program on KKFI featuring music, news, and other programming geared towards the gay and lesbian community. The original pilot aired in January 1989.[234] (June)
2007	Twentieth nnual A.I.D.S. Walk (April)

2007   Gay domestic partnerships are legalized in the states of Washington, Oregon, Colorado, Ohio, and Iowa banning discrimination based on sexual orientation or gender identity in the private sector. On August 9, LOGO hosts the first presidential forum in the United States focusing specifically on LGBT issues. Six Democratic Party candidates participate in the event, including Democratic nominee Barack Obama.[235] (July 22)

2007   "Gay history on view at the Smithsonian," a collection of artifacts from renowned gay activist Frank Kameny, is on display in the Smithsonian National Museum of American History in Washington, D.C.

The Frank Kameny Collection includes such objects as the protest signs from the 1960s demonstrations in Washington and Philadelphia, gay rights buttons with Kameny's famous phrase "Gay is Good" and a photograph of protesters picketing in front of the White House on Oct. 23, 1965, which Kameny helped organize.

GAY IS GOOD

"This is the first time the Smithsonian has ever included displays of gay civil rights artifacts," said Bob Witeck, CEO of Witeck-Combs Communications, Inc. "This exhibit gives (the gay rights) story equal treatment alongside other movements." Kameny's artifacts will rest in the "Treasures of American History" exhibit alongside such historic American objects as the Greensboro, N.C., lunch counter from the 1960 desegregation protest, the ruby slippers worn by Judy Garland in "The Wizard of Oz," Abraham Lincoln's top hat and Thomas Edison's light bulb.

The Smithsonian describes "Treasures of American History" as representing "the breadth of American history . . . conveying the significance of each object as a treasure of American history." Other objects in this case, titled the New Acquisitions of the National Museum of American History, include a pair of boxing gloves worn and signed by Joe Louis from his fight against Max Schmeling, a teapot reading "No Stamp Act" and a rare photograph of a freed slave wearing an American flag. The exhibit closes Oct. 29.[236] (August)

2007   *Gay Lesbian Bisexual Transgender and Youth Referral Hotline for KS and MO* founded by Jeanne M. Foster (4218 Roanoke Ave Rd Ste 305, Kansas City, Missouri) (formerly Gay Lesbian Bisexual Transgender Youth Crisis Hotline for KS and MO), with Allan Kahn (5631 E US Hwy 40, Kansas City, Missouri); Raymond Jemison (642 N Hocker, Independence, MO); Christian Ethington (3201 Southwest Trwy, Kansas City, Missouri); Connie Spies (3201 Southwest Trfwy, Kansas City, Missouri).[237] (August 14)

2007   *Kansas City Lesbian, Gay and Allied Lawyers* founded with Lana M. Knedlik at Stinson, Morrison, Hecker, LLP (1201 Walnut, Kansas City, Missouri), as registered agent.[238] (October 2)

2008	The civil union law goes into effect in New Hampshire.[239] (January 1)

2008   Domestic partnership legislation in Oregon becomes effective.[240] (February 4)

2008   **Twenty-first annual A.I.D.S. Walk (April)**

2008   California State Supreme Court rules it unconstitutional to deny same-sex couples equal marriage rights, making California the second state to legalize same-sex marriage.[241] (May 15)

2008   Californians pass Proposition 8; a voter-approved marriage amendment excluding gays and lesbians their formerly legal right to marry; 18,000 California gay and lesbian couples had married when it was legal to do so. [As of October 2011, marriage for gay and lesbian couples will not be allowed to resume until state and federal appeals courts decide the fate of Prop 8]. (November 4)

2008   **Passages moved to Trinity United Methodist Church.**

2009   **Mario Canedo (at right) coordinates the first (of what becomes an annual) Latino Gay Pride called Orgullo Latino.**[242]

2009   *The EQUAL Youth Center* was founded out of the
            efforts of *The Phoenix Project* to address the needs
            of queer youth in Kansas City with the goal of
            creating a physical community center for queer
            youth that provides support services and an avenue
            for grassroots LGBT activism. Incorporated March
            24, 2010.[243] (April)

2009   Twenty-second annual A.I.D.S. Walk (April)

2009   Pastor Kurt Krieger was installed as Senior Pastor
            of *Spirit of Hope MCC* on September 20, 2009,
            succeeding Pastor John Barbone as the second
            longest serving MCC reverend in the country.
            The vote to call Kurt was taken on March 13, 2009
            after a lengthy process to study models of
            leadership transition in churches. Pastor Kurt had
            been a member of Spirit of Hope MCC since
            January 1985. Kurt served the church in a variety
            of roles including Minister of Worship, the
            newsletter editor, the chair of a property search
            committee and the conveener of the Council of
            Ministries of *Spirit of Hope MCC*. In 2011, the
            Church donated Phyllis Shafer's "Gays Changing
            Times" scrapbooks for preservation in the Gay and
            Lesbian Archive of Mid-America (GLAMA).[244]

2009   The *Gay and Lesbian Archive of Mid-America*
            (GLAMA) founded by professional archivists and
            curators from the Jackson County Historical
            Society, Kansas City Museum, and LaBudde
            Special Collections of Miller Nichols Library at the
            University of Missouri-Kansas City.

GAY AND LESBIAN ARCHIVE OF MID-AMERICA

A.I.D.S. Walk T-Shirts from 1988-2009, preserved by Terry Newell and Mike Sugnet [who found the first two shirts], was the first collection to be donated to GLAMA. Subsequently, an exhibits-in-print postcard book, *What We Did for Love: AIDS Walk T-Shirt Collection*, was published. GLAMA partners launched http://www.glama.us, and began promoting the collecting initiative.[245] (December 1; World A.I.D.S. Day)

2010   Twenty-third annual A.I.D.S. Walk (April)

2010   First *Kansas City Gay Trolley Tours* hosted by GLAMA and led by Ross Freese.[246] (October)

2010   Diane Stafford, *The Kansas City Star*, reports that Dan Nilsen, founder and CEO of Bishop-McCann, a $46 million Kansas City-based agency that specializes in producing meetings, events and incentive programs, received a $5,000 grant as winner of the 2010 NGLCC/Wells Fargo Business Owner of the Year Award, to help establish the Mid-America Gay and Lesbian Chamber of Commerce (MAGLCC), a new affiliate of the National Gay and Lesbian Chamber of Commerce.[247] (November)

2011   Twenty-fourth annual A.I.D.S. Walk. (April)

2011   Marriage for gay and lesbian couples is legalized in the
              state of New York, becoming the 6th and largest state
              with such legislation. (June 23)

2011   " Don't Ask, Don't Tell" (DADT) is repealed. DADT
              was the official United States policy on homosexuals
              serving in the military from December 21, 1993. The
              policy prohibited military personnel from
              discriminating against or harassing closeted
              homosexual or bisexual service members or
              applicants, while barring openly gay, lesbian, or
              bisexual persons from military service. Barack Obama
              also ordered that the Justice Department stop
              defending in court a law defining marriage as between
              a man and a woman.[248] (September 20)

2011   Second *Kansas City Gay Trolley Tours* is hosted by
              GLAMA, and led by Ross Freese. GLAMA
              celebrated the 45th Anniversary of the historic
              NACHO conference that took place in downtown
              Kansas City in 1966. Drew Shafer's surviving
              partner, Mickey Ray, returned to Kansas City for
              the festivities, and participated in a weekend of
              events.[249] (October 15 and 16)

2011   *OUTFEST: Unity in the Community* provides an
              event for all ages, with an outreach to high school
              and collegiate communities. OUTFest also featured
              workshops (including a lecture by Mickey Ray) and
              another terrific slate of afternoon entertainment
              from drag queen, Belle Starr, and cast, raffle
              drawings throughout the day, and more.[250]
              (October 16)

[1] Sodomy being defined as non-procreative sexual activity, as per the English Common Law tradition of sodomy laws under King Henry VIII in 1533. Information courtesy Ross Freese.

[2] In 1867, August Karl Heinrich Ulrichs, at the Congress of German Jurists in Munich gives a speech for *"Urning"* or homosexual rights which marks the beginning of the public homosexual emancipation movement in Germany. The word Lesbianism appears in an Englishman's diary in 1870; it isn't used as a noun until 1925. "Heterosexualität" appears in print for the 1st time in 1880, 11 years after "Homosexualität." The word 'homosexual' finally appears in English in John Addington Symonds' *A Problem in Modern Ethics*. And, The word "bisexual" is first used in its current sense in Charles Gilbert Chaddock's translation of Kraft-Ebing's *Psychopathia Sexualis* in 1892. Information courtesy Ross Freese.

[3] 1870 Kansas City, Missouri, City Directory, p. 53. Both Gay and Charlotte were likely names of daughters of landowners who platted and subdivided that area.

[4] http://www.pitch.com/fatcity/archives/2011/03/09/oscar-wilde-ate-here-really-he-did (viewed 30 Sept 2011).

[5] http://www.365gay.com/uncategorized/an-american-gay-history-timeline-1903-2008/ (viewed 14 Feb 2011).

[6] http://bama.ua.edu/~safezone/timeline.pdf (viewed 17 Sept 2010).

[7] http://bama.ua.edu/~safezone/timeline.pdf (viewed 17 Sept 2010).

[8] "Roosevelt to all boys: 'Sissies' and 'Bullies' are both to be despised, he says," *Kansas City* (Mo.) *Star*, 26 Nov. 1913, p. 14.

[9] http://bama.ua.edu/~safezone/timeline.pdf (viewed 17 Sept 2010).

[10] http://bama.ua.edu/~safezone/timeline.pdf (viewed 17 Sept 2010).

[11] http://www.365gay.com/uncategorized/an-american-gay-history-timeline-1903-2008/; and. http://bama.ua.edu/~safezone/timeline.pdf (viewed 17 Sept 2010).

[12] http://www.queerculturalcenter.org/Pages/Bentley/QueersinJazz.html (viewed 19 Sept 2011). Also, Haggerty, George E. *Gay Histories and Cultures: An Encyclopedia.*

[13] Paragraph 175 was a provision of the German Criminal Code from May 15, 1871, to March 10, March 1994, that made homosexual acts between males a crime. http://bama.ua.edu/~safezone/timeline.pdf (viewed 17 Sept 2010).

[14] http://bama.ua.edu/~safezone/timeline.pdf (viewed 17 Sept 2010).

[15] http://www.365gay.com/uncategorized/an-american-gay-history-timeline-1903-2008/ (viewed 17 Sept 2010).

[16] http://www.infoplease.com/ipa/A0194028.html; http://en.wikipedia.org/wiki/Mattachine_Society; http://www.365gay.com/uncategorized/an-american-gay-history-timeline-1903-2008/ (viewed 17 Sept 2010).

[17] http://www.onearcH.I.V.es.org/ (viewed 6 Jan 2010).

[18] http://www.infoplease.com/ipa/A0194028.html; http://www.law.fsu.edu/journals/lawreview/frames/244/eskrfram.html (viewed 27 June 2010).

[19] http://www.infoplease.com/ipa/A0194028.html; http://www.365gay.com/uncategorized/an-american-gay-history-timeline-1903-2008/ (viewed 17 Sept 2010).

[20] http://www.glhalloffame.org/index.pl?todo=view_itemanditem=110 (viewed 19 Sept 2011). Foster and her partner at the time, Hazel Tollliver, lived in the Kansas City area for more than a year. First they lived over by KU at 2004 W 41st, Kansas City, Kansas. Then, Tolliver left for a job elsewhere while Foster and Tolliver's mother, Myrtle, lived on Harrison near UMKC. Foster worked on her studies for nearly 30 years. She decided to self-publish in the 1940s after the death of her parents but did not actually publish until 1956 while she was here working at UMKC. Information courtesy Ross Freese.

[21] http://bama.ua.edu/~safezone/timeline.pdf (viewed 17 Sept 2010).

[22] May, Linda. "Women in Kansas City's Heritage," News-Telegraph, March 1992, p. 5; Recollection of Robin Wayne Bailey on GLAMA Facebook (viewed 7 June 2010); http://www.campkc.com/newsite/story/outthere-more-cards-and-gifts (viewed 28 Sept. 2011).

[23] http://www.pitch.com/kansascity/kcs-new-gay-and-lesbian-archive-of-mid-america-remembers-a-pioneer-town/Content?oid=2198838 (viewed 3 June 2010).

[24] http://www.365gay.com/uncategorized/an-american-gay-history-timeline-1903-2008/; http://www.christianliferesources.com/?library/view.phpandarticleid=915(viewed 17 Sept 2010).

[25] Brad Shaw worked at the Jewel Box Lounge years ago designing their outfits. See, "This Is Who I Am: An Interview with Ron Megee, Starring in Unicorn's 'La Cage,'" "Camp," August 2007.

[26] http://www.365gay.com/uncategorized/an-american-gay-history-timeline-1903-2008/ (viewed 17 Sept 2010).

[27] "Homosexual is Group Subject," Kansas City (Mo.) Times, 21 Feb. 1966; Phillips, Scoop. "The Making of a Community," News-Telegraph, March 1992, p. 3; Illinois Secretary of State Charter No. 7642. Newton, David E. *Gay and Lesbian Rights: A Reference Handbook*, 15-16; Foster Gunnison, Jr., Papers, Box 47, Folders 536-538, University of Connecticut, Thomas J. Dodd Research Center, Archives and Special Collections, 405 Babbidge Road Unit 1205, Storrs, CT 06269-1205.

[28] Humphreys, Laud. *Out of the Closets: The Sociology of Homosexual Liberation*. (Englewood Cliffs, NJ: Prentice-Hall, Inc., 1972), p. 114; "Homosexual is Group Subject," Kansas City (Mo.) Times, 21 Feb. 1966; Phillips, Scoop. "The Making of a Community," News-Telegraph, March 1992, p. 3.

[29] Shilts, Randy. *Conduct Unbecoming: Gays and Lesbians in the U. S. Military*. (New York: St. Martin's Press, 2005), 65-66; The Phoenix: Midwest Homophile Voice (August 1967) 2:7: 23.

[30] "Phoenix Rising," *Verge magazine* 2007 (Summer) announcing Gary Miller's donation of a full run of the magazine to the editor of the magazine (To date, we have not been able to locate Mr. Shon Ledbetter, editor of Verge magazine as of

2007, or Jon P. Patterson, President of JP Media Group, when this author first attempted to contact them about archiving "The Phoenix" newsletters.); Foster Gunnison, Jr., Papers, Box 47, Folders 536-538, University of Connecticut, Thomas J. Dodd Research Center, Archives and Special Collections, 405 Babbidge Road Unit 1205, Storrs, CT 06269-1205; Humphreys, Laud. *Out of the Closets: The Sociology of Homosexual Liberation.* (Englewood Cliffs, NJ: Prentice-Hall, Inc., 1972), p. 114.

[31] Foster Gunnison, Jr., Papers, Box 47, Folders 536-538, University of Connecticut, Thomas J. Dodd Research Center, Archives and Special Collections, 405 Babbidge Road Unit 1205, Storrs, CT 06269-1205; Phillips, Scoop. "The Making of a Community," News-Telegraph, March 1992, p. 3 [with some misinformation].

[32] "Phoenix: Midwest Homophile Voice," Kansas City (February), 1967.

[33] "Phoenix: Midwest Homophile Voice," Kansas City (February), 1967.

[34] *New York Times*, 1967.

[35] *The Phoenix: Midwest Homophile Voice* (August 1967) 2:7: 23.

[36] *The Phoenix: Midwest Homophile Voice* (August 1967) 2:7: 23.

[37] Phillips, Scoop. "The Making of a Community," News-Telegraph, March 1992, p. 3; http://www.mickeyray.com/bio.asp (viewed 5 Jan 2010); Humphreys, Laud. *Out of the Closets: The Sociology of Homosexual Liberation.* (Englewood Cliffs, NJ: Prentice-Hall, Inc., 1972), p. 114.

[38] May, Linda. "Women in Kansas City's Heritage," *News-Telegraph*, March 1992, p. 5.

[39] http://en.wikipedia.org/wiki/The_Ladder_%28magazine%29 (viewed 19 Sept 2011).

[40] Phillips, Scoop. "The Making of a Community," *News-Telegraph*, March 1992, p. 3.

[41] Illinois Secretary of State Charter No. 7642; http://www.mickeyray.com/phoenix-society.asp (viewed 19 April 2010). D'Emilio, John. *Sexual Politics, Sexual Communities: The Making of a Homosexual Minority in the United States, 1940-1970.* (Chicago: University of Illinois Press, 1983), 199; Foster Gunnison, Jr., Papers, Box 47, Folders 536-538, University of Connecticut, Thomas J. Dodd Research Center, Archives and Special Collections, 405 Babbidge Road Unit 1205, Storrs, CT 06269-1205.

[42] Phillips, Scoop. "The Making of a Community," *News-Telegraph*, March 1992, p. 3.

[43] *Kansas City* (Mo.) *Star* (or *Times*), 31 Oct. 1968; and, "Vital Clue from Man Thought Dead," *Kansas City* (Mo.) *Times*, 12 Dec. 1968. Also, Phyllis Shafer Scrapbook Collection, Scrapbook I, Gay and Lesbian Archives of Mid-America (GLAMA).

[44] http://www.mickeyray.com/bio.asp; http://www.mickeyray.com/shafer.asp (viewed 11 Jan 2010).

[45] "Los Angeles: Metropolitan Community Church: Homosexuals Form their own Church," by Edward E. Fiske, *New York Times*, 21 Feb. 1970.

[46] http://bama.ua.edu/~safezone/timeline.pdf (viewed 17 Sept 2010).

[47] http://www.365gay.com/uncategorized/an-american-gay-history-timeline-1903-2008/; http://www.infoplease.com/ipa/A0194028.html (viewed 17 Sept 2010).

[48] Phillips, Scoop. "The Making of a Community," *News-Telegraph*, March 1992,

p. 3; "Few Know World of Gay Women: NACHO This Week," *Kansas City* (Mo.) *Star*, 29 Aug. 1969, p. 8; "Gay role quieter in KC's past," *Kansas City* (Mo.) *Star*, 20 Mar. 1994, A13.

[49] Phillips, Scoop. "The Making of a Community," *News-Telegraph*, March 1992, p. 3.

[50] Phillips, Scoop. "The Making of a Community," *News-Telegraph*, March 1992, p. 3; "Gay role quieter in KC's past," *Kansas City* (Mo.) *Star*, 20 Mar. 1994, A13.

[51] Phillips, Scoop. "The Making of a Community," *News-Telegraph*, March 1992, p. 3.

[52] Or, Womantown, as mentioned in, "Snapshots of our Past: Reflections on Kansas City's Gay History," by Sarah Ivy, *Verge Magazine*, Volume 3; http://www.pitch.com/kansascity/kcs-new-gay-and-lesbian-archive-of-mid-america-remembers-a-pioneer-town/Content?oid=2198838 (viewed 19 Sept 2011).

[53] Newton, David E. *Gay and Lesbian Rights: A Reference Handbook*, 15-16.

[54] Phillips, Scoop. "The Making of a Community," *News-Telegraph*, March 1992, p. 3; Humphreys, Laud. *Out of the Closets: The Sociology of Homosexual Liberation*. (Englewood Cliffs, NJ: Prentice-Hall, Inc., 1972), p. 114-115.

[55] Humphreys, Laud. *Out of the Closets: The Sociology of Homosexual Liberation*. (Englewood Cliffs, NJ: Prentice-Hall, Inc., 1972), p. 114

[56] An unidentified Colorado Springs, Colorado, newspaper dated 29 June 1970.

[57] *The News*, 11 Sept. 1970.

[58] Missouri Secretary of State Charter No. N00010751.

[59] *Kansas City* (Mo.) *Times*, 8 Dec. 1970.

[60] http://www.365gay.com/uncategorized/an-american-gay-history-timeline-1903-2008/ (viewed 17 Sept 2010).

[61] "Snapshots of our Past: Reflections on Kansas City's Gay History," by Sarah Ivy, *Verge Magazine*, Volume 3. Gerry Young added that, *"After Congress approved the ERA it was sent to the states for ratification. In 1982 the ERA quietly died after 10 years on the table, just 3 states shy of ratification; it never passed in Missouri or Kansas."*

[62] Phillips, Scoop. "The Making of a Community," *News-Telegraph*, March 1992, p. 3; also, "He's Read Leviticus: Founder of Gay Church Argues for Tolerance," *Kansas City* (Mo.) *Star* (or *Times*?), 27 Aug. 1973; *Kansas City* (Mo.) *Star*, 16 Oct. 1976.

[63] "Snapshots of our Past: Reflections on Kansas City's Gay History," by Sarah Ivy, *Verge Magazine*, Volume 3; and, Phyllis Shafer Scrapbook Collection, Scrapbook II, Gay and Lesbian Archives of Mid-America (GLAMA).

[64] http://www.365gay.com/uncategorized/an-american-gay-history-timeline-1903-2008/; http://bama.ua.edu/~safezone/timeline.pdf (viewed 17 Sept 2010). Also, Phyllis Shafer Scrapbook Collection, Scrapbook I, [p. 61], Gay and Lesbian Archives of Mid-America (GLAMA).

[65] "Snapshots of our Past: Reflections on Kansas City's Gay History," by Sarah Ivy, *Verge Magazine*, Volume 3.

[66] Missouri Secretary of State Charter No. N00014987.

[67] Phillips, Scoop. "The Making of a Community," *News-Telegraph*, March 1992,

p. 3; Missouri Secretary of State Charter No. N00015015.

[68] *Kansas City* (Mo.) *Star* (or *Times*?), 7 Apr. 1974, from Phyllis Shafer Scrapbook Collection, Scrapbook I, [p. 59-60], Gay and Lesbian Archives of Mid-America (GLAMA). See also, "Gay role quieter in KC's past," *Kansas City* (Mo.) *Star*, 20 Mar. 1994, A13.

[69] AT: Alchoholics Together at MCC publication in Phyllis Shafer Scrapbook Collection, Scrapbook I, Gay and Lesbian Archives of Mid-America (GLAMA).

[70] Phyllis Shafer Scrapbook Collection, Scrapbook II, Gay and Lesbian Archives of Mid-America (GLAMA).

[71] http://www.365gay.com/uncategorized/an-american-gay-history-timeline-1903-2008/ (viewed 17 Sept 2010).

[72] Phillips, Scoop. "The Making of a Community," *News-Telegraph*, March 1992, p. 3.

[73] "Snapshots of our Past: Reflections on Kansas City's Gay History," by Sarah Ivy, *Verge Magazine*, Volume 3.

[74] *Kansas City* (Mo.) *Star*, 2 Apr. 1975, p. 1Aand1B. Also, Phyllis Shafer Scrapbook Collection, Scrapbook I, Gay and Lesbian Archives of Mid-America (GLAMA).

[75] *Kansas City* (Mo.) *Star*, 3 Apr. 1975, p. 1, 12; also, Phyllis Shafer Scrapbook Collection, Scrapbook I, [p. 61-62], Gay and Lesbian Archives of Mid-America (GLAMA).

[76] St. Louis Post-Dispatch, undated; also Phyllis Shafer Scrapbook Collection, Scrapbook I, [p. 61], Gay and Lesbian Archives of Mid-America (GLAMA).

[77] *Kansas City* (Mo.) *Star*, 4 Apr. 1975, 7A. Also, Phyllis Shafer Scrapbook Collection, Scrapbook I, Gay and Lesbian Archives of Mid-America (GLAMA).

[78] Phyllis Shafer Scrapbook Collection, Scrapbook I, p. 36, Gay and Lesbian Archives of Mid-America (GLAMA).

[79] *Kansas City* (Mo.) *Star*, 23 Oct. 1975.

[80] May, Linda. "Women in Kansas City's Heritage," *News-Telegraph*, March 1992, p. 5.

[81] May, Linda. "Women in Kansas City's Heritage," *News-Telegraph*, March 1992, p. 5.

[82] May, Linda. "Women in Kansas City's Heritage," *News-Telegraph*, March 1992, p. 5.

[83] Phillips, Scoop. "The Making of a Community," *News-Telegraph*, March 1992, p. 3; Missouri Secretary of State Charter No. N00015015.

[84] Phillips, Scoop. "The Making of a Community," *News-Telegraph*, March 1992, p. 3.

[85] Minister to City's Homosexuals, *Kansas City* (Mo.) *Star*, 30 Jan. 1977, p. 2C. Also, Phyllis Shafer Scrapbook Collection, Scrapbook I, Gay and Lesbian Archives of Mid-America (GLAMA).

[86] Phillips, Scoop. "The Making of a Community," *News-Telegraph*, March 1992, p. 3. Also, Craft, Cindy, "Play Ball!" *News-Telegraph*, March 1992, p. 9.

[87] *Kansas City* (Mo.) *Star*, 16 Oct. 1976.

[88] Phyllis Shafer Scrapbook Collection, Scrapbook I, [p. 50-54], Gay and Lesbian Archives of Mid-America (GLAMA).

[89] *Kansas City* (Mo.) *Star*, 18 Aug. 1976.

[90] *Kansas City* (Mo.) *Times*, 19 Aug. 1976.

[91] *Kansas City* (Mo.) *Times*, 20 Aug. 1976.

[92] *Chicago Tribune*, 22 Aug. 1976, p. 1.

[93] *Kansas City* (Mo.) *Star* (or *Times*?), 17 Oct. 1976. Also, Phyllis Shafer Scrapbook Collection, Scrapbook I, Gay and Lesbian Archives of Mid-America (GLAMA).

[94] *Kansas City* (Mo.) *Times*, 19 Nov. 1976. Also, Phyllis Shafer Scrapbook Collection, Scrapbook I, Gay and Lesbian Archives of Mid-America (GLAMA).

[95] "Minister to City's Homosexuals," *Kansas City* (Mo.) *Star,* 30 Jan. 1977, p. 2C. Also, Phyllis Shafer Scrapbook Collection, Scrapbooks I and II, Gay and Lesbian Archives of Mid-America (GLAMA).

[96] AT: Alchoholics Together at MCC publication in Phyllis Shafer Scrapbook Collection, Scrapbook I, Gay and Lesbian Archives of Mid-America (GLAMA).

[97] *Schenectady Gazette*, 27 June 1977, p. 1.

[98] Phillips, Scoop. "The Making of a Community," *News-Telegraph*, March 1992, p. 3. *Kansas City Star/Times* coverage, 13 and 15 July 1977 (where the Times reported, *"The greater threat to this society, which struggles toward justice for all, is not the ordinary homosexual; it is the Anita Bryant's who catch up so many gullible and unsophisticated Americans in their messianic madness."* Also, 17 June 1978; and, Phyllis Shafer Scrapbook Collection, Scrapbook I, Gay and Lesbian Archives of Mid-America (GLAMA).

[99] Phillips, Scoop. "The Making of a Community," *News-Telegraph*, March 1992, p. 3. Another source said the first parade was in 1973, but did not provide substantiation. See, "Gay role quieter in KC's past," *Kansas City* (Mo.) *Star*, 20 Mar. 1994, A13.

[100] *Kansas City* (Mo.) *Star*, 24 July 1977. Also, Phyllis Shafer Scrapbook Collection, Scrapbook I, Gay and Lesbian Archives of Mid-America (GLAMA).

[101] *Kansas City* (Mo.) *Star*, 6 Aug. 1977 (also, "Opinions by Schneiders Bring Homosexuals good, Bad News," by Randall W. Myers, p. 3B). Also, Phyllis Shafer Scrapbook Collection, Scrapbook I, Gay and Lesbian Archives of Mid-America (GLAMA).

[102] May, Linda. "Women in Kansas City's Heritage," *News-Telegraph*, March 1992, p. 5; https://www.sos.mo.gov/BusinessEntity/soskb/Corp.asp?655576 (viewed 22 Nov 2010).

[103] *Kansas City* (Mo.) *Times*, 8 Sept. 1977.

[104] AT: Alchoholics Together at MCC publication in Phyllis Shafer Scrapbook Collection, Scrapbooks I and II, Gay and Lesbian Archives of Mid-America (GLAMA).

[105] *Kansas City* (Mo.) *Times*, 4 Oct. 1977. See also, "Cartoons: Homosexuality Ain't Normal," *Kansas City* (Mo.) *Star* (or *Times*?), 6 Oct. 1977; and, "Opinions," on 9 Oct., 14 Oct., and 19 Oct. 1977. Also in Phyllis Shafer Scrapbook Collection, Scrapbook I, Gay and Lesbian Archives of Mid-America (GLAMA); and, http://en.wikipedia.org/wiki/LGBT_rights_in_the_United_States (viewed 18 Mar 2011).

[106] *Kansas City* (Mo.) *Star*, 10 Oct. 1977. Also, Phyllis Shafer Scrapbook Collection, Scrapbook I, Gay and Lesbian Archives of Mid-America (GLAMA).

[107] *Kansas City* (Mo.) *Star*, 15 Oct. 1977. See also, "Opinions," and "City Human Relations Committee," *Kansas City* (Mo.) *Times*, 25 Oct. 1977; Also, Phyllis Shafer Scrapbook Collection, Scrapbook I, Gay and Lesbian Archives of Mid-America (GLAMA).

[108] *Kansas City* (Mo.) *Star*, 24 Oct. 1977 (and, "New Church Look at Homosexuality," *Kansas City* (Mo.) *Times*, 24 Oct. 1977; and, "Church Seek Jewish Dialogue," *Kansas City* (Mo.) *Times*, 25 Oct. 1977; also, Phyllis Shafer Scrapbook Collection, Scrapbook I, Gay and Lesbian Archives of Mid-America (GLAMA).

[109] *Kansas City* (Mo.) *Star* (or *Times*?), 17 Nov. 1977; also, "Gays and Anti-Gays Turn Out in Full Force," by Ron Lee, *Columbia* (Mo.) *Daily Tribune*, 22 Nov. 1977; "Gay Activists Brush Shoulders with Opponents," by Betty Connor and Timothy O'Harin, *Columbia* (Mo.) *Missourian*; also, Phyllis Shafer Scrapbook Collection, Scrapbook I, Gay and Lesbian Archives of Mid-America (GLAMA).

[110] *Kansas City* (Mo.) *Star Magazine*, 20 Nov. 1977; also, Phyllis Shafer Scrapbook Collection, Scrapbook I, Gay and Lesbian Archives of Mid-America (GLAMA).

[111] Phillips, Scoop. "The Making of a Community," *News-Telegraph*, March 1992, p. 3

[112] May, Linda. "Women in Kansas City's Heritage," *News-Telegraph*, March 1992, p. 5

[113] http://supreme.justia.com/us/434/1080/case.html (viewed 19 June 2011); "UM Loses Appeal in Gay's Lawsuit," *Kansas City* (Mo.) *Star*, 21 Feb. 1978, and "Without University Harassment Gay Rights Group Flourishing," *Kansas City* (Mo.) *Star*, 6 Mar. 1978; "Gay Students Now Recognized," by K. R. Kamphoefner, Gay Student Union, *The University News*, 14 Sept. 1978; also, Phyllis Shafer Scrapbook Collection, Scrapbook I, Gay and Lesbian Archives of Mid-America (GLAMA).

[114] Phillips, Scoop. "The Making of a Community," *News-Telegraph*, March 1992, p. 3; "Gay Pride Parade Set for June 16 Downtown," *Kansas City* (Mo.) *Times*, 17 June 1978; also, Phyllis Shafer Scrapbook Collection, Scrapbook I, Gay and Lesbian Archives of Mid-America (GLAMA).

[115] "Steppin Out Opens Doors," *Kansas City* (Mo.) *Star*, 9 Nov. 1978; also Phyllis Shafer Scrapbook Collection, Scrapbook I, Gay and Lesbian Archives of Mid-America (GLAMA).

[116] *Kansas City* (Mo.) *Star* (or *Times*?), 27 Nov. 1978; also, Phyllis Shafer Scrapbook Collection, Scrapbook II, Gay and Lesbian Archives of Mid-America (GLAMA).

[117] http://bama.ua.edu/~safezone/timeline.pdf (viewed 17 Sept 2010).

[118] Phillips, Scoop. "The Making of a Community," *News-Telegraph*, March 1992, p. 3; *Spectrum*, 9 July 1979; also, Phyllis Shafer Scrapbook Collection, Scrapbook II, Gay and Lesbian Archives of Mid-America (GLAMA).

[119] Missouri Secretary of State Charter No. N00023263.

[120] Phillips, Scoop. "The Making of a Community," *News-Telegraph*, March 1992, p. 3; "Snapshots of our Past: Reflections on Kansas City's Gay History," by Sarah Ivy, *Verge Magazine*, Volume 3.

[121] *Kansas City* (Mo.) *Star*, 20 May 1980; also also, Phyllis Shafer Scrapbook Collection, Scrapbook II, Gay and Lesbian Archives of Mid-America (GLAMA).

[122] Phillips, Scoop. "The Making of a Community," *News-Telegraph*, March 1992, p. 3.

[123] http://bama.ua.edu/~safezone/timeline.pdf (viewed 17 Sept 2010).

[124] Craft, Cindy. "Play Ball!" *News-Telegraph*, March 1992, p. 9.

[125] http://www.365gay.com/uncategorized/an-american-gay-history-timeline-1903-2008/ (viewed 24 Aug 2010); Steve Metzler Kansas City Museum's Community Curator Program on http://www.youtube.com/user/kansascitymuseum; http://en.wikipedia.org/wiki/AIDS (viewed 19 Sept. 2011).

[126] Phillips, Scoop. "The Making of a Community," *News-Telegraph*, March 1992, p. 3.

[127] *The Palm Beach Post*, 18 May 1981, p. 9.

[128] Phillips, Scoop. "The Making of a Community," *News-Telegraph*, March 1992, p. 3.

[129] St. *Louis Journalism Review*, Sept. 1995. Also, "10 YEARS AFTER: Editor Jim Thomas Celebrates A Decade Of The Gay News-Telegraph," by Ellen Futterman, *St. Louis Post-Dispatch*, 29 Sept. 1991.

[130] Phillips, Scoop. "The Making of a Community," *News-Telegraph,* March 1992, p. 3. The next parade that the author could locate was more than a decade later in 1998.

[131] http://www.365gay.com/uncategorized/an-american-gay-history-timeline-1903-2008/ (viewed 24 Aug 2010).

[132] http://www.365gay.com/uncategorized/an-american-gay-history-timeline-1903-2008/ (viewed 24 Aug 2010).

[133] "Church Offers Haven for Gay Christians," *Kansas City* (Mo.) *Star*, 29 June 1982, B1, 6; also Phyllis Shafer Scrapbook Collection, Scrapbook II, Gay and Lesbian Archives of Mid-America (GLAMA).

[134] "Disease Afflicting Homosexuals Reported in Kansas City," by Tom Ramstock, *Kansas City* (Mo.) *Times*, 14 Oct. 1982; Steve Metzler Kansas City Museum's Program on http://www.youtube.com/user/kansascitymuseum; m"Snapshots of our Past: Reflections on Kansas City's Gay History," by Sarah Ivy, *Verge Magazine*, Volume 3.

[135] Phyllis Shafer Scrapbook Collection, Scrapbook II, Gay and Lesbian Archives of Mid-America (GLAMA).

[136] Craft, Cindy. "Play Ball!" *News-Telegraph*, March 1992, p. 9.

[137] Another source said Gay Talk for peer counseling debuted in 1976. See, "Gay role quieter in KC's past," *Kansas City* (Mo.) *Star*, 20 Mar. 1994, A13.

[138] Phillips, Scoop. "The Making of a Community," *News-Telegraph*, March 1992, p. 3.

[139] *Newsweek*, 8 Aug. 1983.

[140] Steve Metzler Kansas City Museum's Community Curator Program on http://www.youtube.com/user/kansascitymuseum.

[141] Missouri Secretary of State Charter No. N00030915.

[142] http://www.gsp-kc.org/about.aspx?id=32 (viewed 19 July 2011). Missouri Secretary of State Charter No. N00031120; http://www.sos.mo.gov/kbimaging/12882069.pdf (viewed 19 July 2011); http://www.sos.mo.gov/kbimaging/12882059.pdf (viewed 19 July 2011); Steve Metzler Kansas City Museum's Community Curator Program on http://www.youtube.com/user/kansascitymuseum.

[143] "Snapshots of our Past: Reflections on Kansas City's Gay History," by Sarah Ivy, *Verge Magazine*, Volume 3.

[144] Missouri Secretary of State Charter No. N00031184.

[145] Phillips, Scoop. "The Making of a Community," *News-Telegraph*, March 1992, p. 3.

[146] *Kansas City* (Mo.) *Times*, 17 Aug. 1984; also also Phyllis Shafer Scrapbook Collection, Scrapbook II, Gay and Lesbian Archives of Mid-America (GLAMA).

[147] *Kansas City Magazine*, August 1984, Vol 9, No 8.

[148] Phillips, Scoop. "The Making of a Community," *News-Telegraph*, March 1992, p. 3.

[149] http://www.365gay.com/uncategorized/an-american-gay-history-timeline-1903-2008/; http://en.wikipedia.org/wiki/Rock_Hudson (viewed 13 Mar 2010).

[150] http://web.arcH.I.V.e.org/web/20041030071403/vergekc.com/vol3/feature_kcfacesofpride.php?vol=3 (viewed 12 Nov 2010).

[151] http://www.hmckc.org/about/About.aspx (viewed 22 July 2011).

[152] Phillips, Scoop. "The Making of a Community," *News-Telegraph*, March 1992, p. 3.

[153] *Alternate News*, 20 Mar 1987.

[154] http://www.saveinckc.org/; http://www.sos.mo.gov/imaging/22651654.pdf; http://saveinckc.org/content/History (viewed 19 Sept 2011).

[155] *Alternate News*, 20 Mar 1987.

[156] Steve Metzler Kansas City Museum's Community Curator Program on http://www.youtube.com/user/kansascitymuseum.

[157] Steve Metzler Kansas City Museum's Community Curator Program on http://www.youtube.com/user/kansascitymuseum.

[158] Phillips, Scoop. "The Making of a Community," *News-Telegraph*, March 1992, p. 3.

[159] *Alternate News*, 20 Mar 1987, contributed by Robin Wayne through the GLAMA Facebook page.

[160] Speech of Stuart Hinds to the Missouri Valley Room Speakers' Series introducing GLAMA, June 2011.

[161] Phillips, Scoop. "The Making of a Community," *News-Telegraph*, March 1992, p. 3.

[162] *Alternate News*, 23 Oct. 1987; also, also Phyllis Shafer Scrapbook Collection, Scrapbook II, Gay and Lesbian Archives of Mid-America (GLAMA).

[163] Steve Metzler Kansas City Museum's Community Curator Program on http://www.youtube.com/user/kansascitymuseum.

[164] Phillips, Scoop. "The Making of a Community," *News-Telegraph*, March 1992, p. 3; based on http://www.A.I.D.S.walkkansascity.org/ 22nd annual in 2010 (viewed on 23 April 2010); Steve Metzler Kansas City Museum's Community Curator Program on http://www.youtube.com/user/kansascitymuseum.

[165] *Camp*, June 2006, p. 13.

[166] http://www.campkc.com/newsite/story/outthere-more-cards-and-gifts (viewed 28 Sept. 2011). Still operational as of May 2006; OutThere is closed as of this printing.

[167] Steve Metzler Kansas City Museum's Community Curator Program on http://www.youtube.com/user/kansascitymuseum.

[168] http://www.mickeyray.com/shafer.asp (viewed 24 Jan 2010).

[169] Missouri Secretary of State Charter No. N00042590.

[170] Phillips, Scoop. "The Making of a Community," *News-Telegraph*, March 1992, p. 3.

[171] Phillips, Scoop. "The Making of a Community," *News-Telegraph*, March 1992, p. 3.

[172] Phillips, Scoop. "The Making of a Community," *News-Telegraph*, March 1992, p. 3.

[173] Missouri Secretary of State Charter No. N00042140. This merger was filed in May 1990.

[174] May, Linda. "Women in Kansas City's Heritage," *News-Telegraph*, March 1992, p. 5.

[175] Missouri Secretary of State Charter No. X00227718.

[176] *Kansas City* (Mo.) *Star*, 14 June 1991 p. 1C.

[177] http://www.lgcc-kc.org/AboutUs014000000.htm (viewed 24 April 2010).

[178] Craft, Cindy. "Play Ball!" *News-Telegraph*, March 1992, p. 9.

[179] *Kansas City* (Mo.) *Star*, 16 May 1992, p. C3.

[180] *St. Louis Post-Dispatch*, 13 Dec. 1992, p. 1A.

[181] http://www.sos.mo.gov/imaging/6180314.pdf (viewed 19 Aug 2010); Steve Metzler Kansas City Museum's Community Curator Program on http://www.youtube.com/user/kansascitymuseum.

[182] Steve Metzler Kansas City Museum's Community Curator Program on http://www.youtube.com/user/kansascitymuseum; http://www.americanrhetoric.com/speeches/maryfisher1992rnc.html (viewed 16 Aug 2011).

[183] *Kansas City* (Mo.) *Star*, 14 Nov. 1992, p. C6.

[184] *St. Louis Post-Dispatch*, 13 Dec. 1992, p. 1A.

[185] Steve Metzler Kansas City Museum's Community Curator Program on http://www.youtube.com/user/kansascitymuseum.

[186] http://www.365gay.com/uncategorized/an-american-gay-history-timeline-1903-2008/ (viewed 13 Mar 2010).

[187] *Kansas City* (Mo.) *Star*, 6 Feb 1993, p. A1.

[188] *Kansas City* (Mo.) *Star*, 7 Feb 1993, p. A1.

[189] Missouri Secretary of State Charter No. X00253377.

[190] *Kansas City* (Mo.) *Star*, 23 April 1993, p. C1.

[191] *Kansas City* (Mo.) *Star*, 21 July 1993, p. C6.

[192] https://www.sos.mo.gov/businessentity/soskb/Corp.asp?995640 (viewed 30 Sept 2011).

[193] http://www.kcmo.org/CKCMO/Depts/CityManagersOffice/HumanRelations Division/HistoryoftheHumanRightsCommission/index.htm (Viewed 24 Sept 2011).

[194] "Gay role quieter in KC's past," *Kansas City* (Mo.) *Star*, 20 Mar. 1994, A13.

[195] http://www.missiebs.com/index.cfm?page=aboutandsite=A (viewed on 19 Sept 2011).

[196] *Camp*, June 2009.

[197] *Kansas City* (Mo.) *Star*, 27 June 1994, p. A1.

[198] http://en.wikipedia.org/wiki/Tim_Van_Zandt (viewed 20 Oct 2010).

[199] Missouri Secretary of State Charter No. N00051839.

[200] http://www.365gay.com/uncategorized/an-american-gay-history-timeline-1903-2008/ (viewed 17 Sept 2010).

[201] http://www.campkc.com/newsite/story/bird-still-flies-high

[202] http://www.365gay.com/uncategorized/an-american-gay-history-timeline-1903-2008/ (viewed 17 Sept 2010).

[203] Missouri Secretary of State Charter No. N00058096.

[204] *Kansas City* (Mo.) *Star*, 12 Feb. 1998, p. A17.

[205] *Pitch Weekly*, March, 5-11 , 1998, p. 7.

[206] *Kansas City* (Mo.) *Star*, 7 June 1998, p.B1.

[207] *Pitch Weekly*, July 9-15, 1998, p. 6.

[208] http://www.sos.mo.gov/kbimaging/22909400.pdf (viewed 19 Sept 2011).

[209] http://www.365gay.com/uncategorized/an-american-gay-history-timeline-1903-2008/; http://en.wikipedia.org/wiki/Matthew_Shepard (viewed 17 Sept 2010).

[210] http://www.kcgayfilmfest.com/ (viewed 19 Sept 2011).

[211] http:// www.kcwomenschorus.org/ (viewed 19 Sept 2011).

[212] *Pitch Weekly*, June 24-30, 1999, p. 7.

[213] *Pitch Weekly*, August 12-18, 1999, p. 19, 22.

[214] http://web.arcH.I.V.e.org/web/20041030071403/vergekc.com/vol3/feature_kcfacesofpride.php?vol=3 (viewed 12 Mar 2010).

[215] http://www.365gay.com/uncategorized/an-american-gay-history-timeline-1903-2008/ (viewed 17 Sept 2010).

[216] http://www.gaytalk.org (viewed 13 Dec 2010).

[217] *Pitch Weekly*, April 20-26, 2000.

[218] *Pitch Weekly*, July 27-August 2, 2000, p. 22.

[219] *Pitch Weekly*, October 12-18, 2000.

[220] *Kansas City* (Mo.) *Star*, 20 Jan. 2001.

[221] http://kcmafa.org (viewed 18 June 2011).

[222] Steve Metzler Kansas City Museum's Community Curator Program on http://www.youtube.com/user/kansascitymuseum.

[223] *Nevada Daily Mail*, 24 Apr. 2003, p. 24.

[224] http://www.kcavp.org (viewed 19 Feb 2011).

[225] http://www.umkc.edu/lgbt/LGBTQIA/About.html (viewed 19 Sept 2011).

[226] http://www.sos.mo.gov/imaging/8766672.pdf; http://www.gaypridekc.com/AboutUs.php (viewed 9 Nov 2010).

[227] http://www.365gay.com/uncategorized/an-american-gay-history-timeline-1903-2008/ (viewed 17 Septe 2010).

[228] http://www.365gay.com/uncategorized/an-american-gay-history-timeline-1903-2008/ (viewed 17 Sept 2010).

[229] http://www.365gay.com/uncategorized/an-american-gay-history-timeline-1903-2008/ (viewed 17 Sept 2010).

[230] http://www.latimes.com/news/local/la-gmtimeline-fl,0,5345296.htmlstory (viewed 22 May 2011).

[231] http://www.365gay.com/uncategorized/an-american-gay-history-timeline-1903-2008/ (viewed 17 Sept 2010).

[232] *The University News*, 16 Oct. 2006.

[233] *The University News*, 16 Oct. 2006.

[234] *Camp*, June 2006, p. 13.

[235] http://www.365gay.com/uncategorized/an-american-gay-history-timeline-1903-2008/ (viewed 17 Sept 2010).

[236] *The Advocate*, August 2007.

[237] Missouri Secretary of State Charter No. N00836008.

[238] Missouri Secretary of State Charter No. N00846204.

[239] http://www.365gay.com/uncategorized/an-american-gay-history-timeline-1903-2008/ (viewed 17 Sept 2010).

[240] http://www.365gay.com/uncategorized/an-american-gay-history-timeline-1903-2008/ (viewed 17 Sept 2010).

[241] http://www.365gay.com/uncategorized/an-american-gay-history-timeline-1903-2008/ (viewed 17 Sept 2010).

[242] http://www.campkc.com/campkc-content.php?Page_ID=1708 (viewed 28 Sept 2011).

[243] http://www.equalcenter.org/about.html; http://www.sos.mo.gov/imaging/25214549.pdf (viewed 22 May 2011).

[244] http://www.campkc.com/campkc-content.php?Page_ID=1240; also, http://www.spiritofhopemcckc.org/ (viewed 1 Oct. 2011).

[245] GLAMA administrative files.

[246] GLAMA administrative files.

[247] http://www.nglcc.org (viewed 19 Sept. 2011).

[248] http://www.kansascity.com/2011/09/19/3152546/pentagon-ready-for-gay-ban-repeal.html (viewed 19 Sept. 2011).

[249] GLAMA administrative files.

[250] http://www.gaypridekc.com/index.php (viewed 19 Sept. 2011).

CHANGING TIMES

CHAPTER 2

Phoenix Rises after 45 Years:
Drew Shafer and
Phoenix Society for Individual Freedom

by Mickey Ray
(aka. Michael A. Pfleger)

2011 marks the 45th Anniversary of the first-ever, national conference, when lesbian and gay organizations from across the United States met in the Hotel State (aka The Stats) in downtown Kansas City in 1966. The Gay and Lesbian Archive of Mid-America (GLAMA) hosted events commemorating this auspicious anniversary in October 2011 (Gay History Month).

This article touches on the lives of three Kansas City pioneer activists for equal rights for lesbian, gay, bisexual and transgender (LGBT) individuals, Mickey Ray, his life-partner, Drew Shafer, and Drew's mother, Phyllis Shafer, and is based, in part, on text published by Ray at mickeyray.com]

THE MICKEY RAY SHOW

In my childhood I never played 'dress-up,' or pretended I was a girl, although that's not something unusual for either well-adjusted gay or straight boys to experience in their youth.

There was a time during one of those family gatherings when grandparents, aunts, uncles, cousins, my sister, brother and, of course my mom, were assembled, and "Uncle Bill" (I think he was a family friend that we called 'Uncle,' a common denotation for male grown-ups during my youth) made the claim that he could hypnotize people. He asked for volunteers and the next thing I knew, we kids became the subjects of his hypnosis experiment.

Being the actor of the family, even at the tender age of eight, I was ready to perform under any circumstances. And to everyone's astonishment, while none of the other kids seemed to go under his *spell*, little Mickey fell into a deep, hypnotic sleep.

Uncle Bill had me do many of the usual parlor tricks: hold out my arm; smell rotten things that weren't there; and, he even suggested to me that I was now a little girl, and my name was Mary Jane. He instructed me to go over to my Grandpa and tell him my name. I nearly blew it (actually, I'm sure I did) when I walked over to him and forgot the name I was told to repeat. Subsequently, I walked back to our mesmerist, and asked him, "What's my name?" At that point I have no doubt that all the grown-ups realized I was faking it...and they weren't about to let me get away with it.

It was only around 7:30 p.m.; but, it was hypnotically suggested that I was very sleepy and needed to go to bed. My little brain was reeling with protest. I knew I couldn't dare let on without also giving away my pretense, however. I left the living room obediently, and went to my bed. Once my head hit the pillow, I began to cry. At that point, I was told it was alright and that I could now 'wake up,' and come back out with the rest of the family. Whew!

But, having called myself Mary Jane for an evening was the closest I'd come to reversing my male identity.

A ten year jump! I had graduated high school in 1964, and immediately enlisted in the United States Army. I was guaranteed my MOS in Clinical Psychology at Fort Sam Houston, Texas, after basic training. My plan was to be able to get schooling and a career via. the military. I wasn't scheduled to begin basic training until that September; so, I decided to check out the one place of mystery close to my home in Lake Ronkonkoma, and that I'd heard so many, sexual rumors about...Cherry Grove, Fire Island.

I took the ferry over from Sayville, New York, and when we arrived the boat was greeted by a throng of colorfully dressed men of all shapes and sizes, smiling and welcoming all the passengers as if we were long lost family. I was eighteen-years-old, and overwhelmed by the exuberance of these men who treated me as if they had known me all my life! That day, and the weekend I spent there, was an incredible time in my life. I had met other men 'like me,' and what's more, men who thought I was someone special and treated me so. I was not a particularly handsome young man; but, I was young, slim and well-endowed...three commodities that would get me into several *doors* of the affluent regulars at both The Pines and Cherry Grove. I'd met every exotic type of gay men from full-drag to full-leather, all in one weekend. It was a wonderful and dizzying time of my life that would mark the beginning of my personal acceptance, and how I would deal with my own homosexuality from that point forward.

I returned several times that summer before I went off to Fort Dix for basic training. I got to know several of the establishment owners and the "fun" people, and was damn near brokenhearted when I had to say, "Goodbye."

Fate stepped in, and I wound up being medically discharged from the service almost immediately upon arrival. I was born with crossed eyes at birth, and at twelve had three operations to straighten my eyes. My left eye, however, never had the strength to stay straight and turned in slightly. The vision in that eye was also negligible, and though I could see two of everything, the second image was barely visible, so it never bothered me. However, the medics caught that problem when they used more modern equipment than the 'spoon' they used at Whitehall during my physical. And, because of my previous operations, they said I was ineligible to have any further operations and due to the double vision, no matter how slight, and I could not go on the rifle range. Not being able to shoot a rifle, I was not able to complete basic training, and was summarily, medically discharged. No college, no medical school, no career, and because my stay was so short, no military income.

CHANGING TIMES

After getting out of the U. S. Army, I had a weekend in the Big Apple, and ventured to the *82 Club*, a famous New York impersonation club at that time. I saw my first, professional female impersonation show at that time. I was amazed at how some of the performers looked so much like women, and even more amazed when I found out that the male waiters and bartenders weren't men; but, women dressed like men.

I'd gone back home, went to work as an orderly at Central Islip State Hospital and waited for summer to return and get back to my friends and gay life on Fire Island!

The following year, 1965, I'd met many other gay men who had a lot of effected, typically or stereotypically feminine mannerisms. On Fire Island, many men I had met dressed in drag; but, it was all for fun. Any of the other more psychologically complex sexual and gender identities were beyond my scope of understanding back then. The wild and crazy guys I'd met dressed very elaborately, and were totally surreal.

In time, as you will see, I had my chance to follow in the high-heeled footsteps of these unique entertainers. But first, let me introduce you to the love of my life. He was a wonderful, giving and far-sighted individual who I am very proud to say was my lifetime companion, mentor, and best friend for 21 years.

MEETING DREW SHAFER

There was a politically gay life *before* Stonewall, during which I had a small part to play. I became actively involved because I met a man in 1969, who, three years prior, had started the first gay rights organization in Kansas City, Missouri, the *Phoenix Society for Individual Freedom.*

An only child to Robert A. "Bob" and Phyllis Fay Shafer, Drew Robert Shafer grew up in a white, middle-class, liberal family. Spoiled to the bone by his mother, Drew pretty much got whatever he asked for, and although a loner for much of his childhood, he lived a happy, unfettered, carefree life. He recognized he was gay in his early teens and immediately acted on it. He became less shy. He was tall, lanky and outspoken, and he had a wonderful speaking voice. He found early in life that he was able to get others to see his point-of-view fairly easily. He was very charismatic that way.

His family followed the spiritual practices espoused by the Kansas City-based Unity School of Christianity, which is more of a positive thinking movement, than a religious sect. And, more than anything else, 'positive thinking' defined Drew. Nothing completely discouraged this unique man.

He came out of the proverbial closet wild and willing to try anything at the age of twenty-one. But he was most active in his early twenties, during his college years. His mom ran a boarding house, which was filled with Drew's gay male friends. Her 'boys' adored her, and Mrs. Phyllis Shafer was the queen of the roost, and loved her position.

CHANGING TIMES

It was the 1950s. Pink was in, and Drew wore it a lot. He even had a motorcycle, then later a car, painted pink and white. His high school friends called him *Pinky*.

Shafer home at 1838 E 49th St.. 1940

He held dances in the basement of the family home, and provided entertainment for his friends when there was no place else to go publicly at that time.

By the late 1950s and into the early 1960s, a couple of the local strip joint owners began to realize the money that could be made from gays in Kansas City who wanted a place to dance and party. In a sense, Kansas City was ahead of its time as our gay bars were left alone by law enforcement since they were owned, operated, and protected by straight, Italian "family" through the sixties and early seventies.

Straight, strip bars like the *Yum Yum Club* and *Cat Ballou*, and the gay clubs like *The Jewel Box Lounge* and *The Colony Bar* were all on the strip at Troost Avenue between Linwood Boulevard and 34th Street. *The Arabian Nights* opened (near the present day Costco shopping center in midtown), followed by *The Redhead Lounge* at 39th Street in the Westport.

Kansas City's bar life at that time was pretty hopping. There was no skimping in decor and atmosphere, especially at *The Redhead Lounge*. These were beautiful clubs and catered openly to the gay clientele.

Kansas City's clubs even allowed men to slow dance in one another's arms. Each club provided protection where gays felt safe to be themselves. To show the stark contrast in what was permissible or not, clubs in New York City, Chicago, and other more liberal cities totally banned touching on their gay clubs' dance floors!

Little by little, gays started buying their own bars and the 'families' seemed not to care. They had new interests in properties in the remodeled River Quay area of the River Market in Kansas City. They wound up fighting their own, with bars being blown up and other problems, until they were no longer influential in the city.

Outside the bar scene, however, life was a very different story. Gays were not openly tolerated. Gay people did not even give out their last names, for fear of retribution in their families...in their places of work or even worship. There were often muggings and intolerance by the still conservative element, throughout the city. These increased as the gay establishments became more independent. Police harassment also occurred now and again; but, not frequently or violently.

Drew became a big part of the gay bar scene. He made friends and was well known within every spectrum of LGBT community at that time, which was fairly 'underground.' There were always after-hour parties at Drew's home.

At some point, Drew had become aware of the 'gay movement,' and that 'being gay' was *much* more than just a nightlife lifestyle. But, I cannot be sure what specifically spurned his interest in wanting to become politically involved. He once told me he really just wanted to have a club and have fun. But, his destiny foretold that he would become much more involved.

103

He had, at first, been approached by a California-based organization called *One*, which had invited him to become leader of a Midwest chapter of that organization.

ONE Inc. was created in 1952 by Dorr Legg and Don Slater, in part to produce the nation's first national gay periodical, *ONE Magazine*, not long after gay activism first began in Los Angeles in the late 1940s, and with formation of the *Mattachine Society* in 1950. In 1953, ONE Incorporated became the first gay organization to open a public office.

(Courtesy http://en.wikipedia.org/wiki/ONE_National_Gay_%26_Lesbian_Archives)

Not wanting to be controlled by a larger organization half way across the country, Drew decided to create an independent gay rights organization himself.

Starting out with a handful of friends, he did just that. He found a beautiful, three-story home with basement, on the corner of Linwood Boulevard and The Paseo, and moved the organization in with him. He made his home on the third floor, rented the two small rooms on the second floor, and the *Phoenix Society for Individual Freedom* organization operated out of the first floor, with the 'press room' in the basement.

HOW I DISCOVERED PHOENIX

In 1968, I was on the move, trying to find myself, and where I fit in with this new gay world. I moved from place to place, including six months in Australia. I'd taken off from my native upstate New York around May or June of 1968. I wound up in Chicago, and lived there close to the end of July. I'd heard, through the grapevine that the upcoming Democratic convention, which would be held there in August, was rumored to become a mass riot. Specifically, Mayor Dale was 'out to bash heads.' At 22-years-of-age,

I wanted to keep mine for a while longer; it's not the type of scene I wanted to stick around to see.

I had intended to go to California, but some friends suggested I first check out Kansas City, Missouri.

Hopping on the Greyhound, I got off at the downtown bus station, found a cheap room to let, and set off to explore the city, and find a job. I got a job as a waiter, almost immediately, serving at the Owl Club, a private gentlemen's club within the main Kansas City Club in downtown Kansas City.

New to the area, I wanted to meet other gay men. I literally asked people where I worked if they knew of any 'gay bars' in the downtown or midtown area, close to where I was staying. The only name they repeated was *The Redhead Lounge*. I wound up hiking there the long way around; but, finally found it on Broadway, near 39th Street. I walked into a circular bar with loads of red material and glass beads hanging decorously against the draping with red, flocked wallpaper all around the room. There was almost no one in the bar when I got there, other than Bobby, the bartender. I noted a sign in the men's room that said, "Gays were welcome to come to the Westport Methodist Church," which was very nearby, and to a meeting of gays and lesbians that would be held there that very evening.

Of course, I went. There is some validity in the old expression, *"Where do you meet a nice boy? In church!"* I met a young, blonde, Nordic looking couple, Dale and Donna, whom, I'd found out shortly thereafter, were fraternal twins...and both were gay! Dale told me about an upcoming gay pride picnic that was being hosted that Sunday by the *Phoenix Society for Individual Freedom*. They invited me to meet them at the Society's headquarters, Phoenix House, at the corner of Linwood Boulevard and The Paseo, and go with them on the bus to the picnic, which was to be held at one of the Society's member's private property out in the country.

I had some trouble finding Phoenix House at first on that warm summer day on September 1, 1968. I wasn't expecting it to be such a huge home. Little did I know; but, that day would change my life forever. I met at the picnic that day my one and only life's partner, Drew Robert Shafer. Ten years my senior, he was six foot, two inches of open joy, gentleness and kindness. His loving, doting, and totally supportive mother, Phyllis Shafer, was there, too. The rest is HIStory!

Drew and I immediately began dating; it was love at first sight. I moved into the third floor apartment with Drew in his home at 133 Linwood Boulevard, and followed his footsteps as a gay rights activist for the *Phoenix Society* the summer before the Stonewall Riots.

PHOENIX SOCIETY'S MISSION

In 1966, born out of need for a national coalition of gay and lesbian leaders, the National Planning Conference of Homophile Organizations (NPCHO) was established. This first-ever, truly national coalition of LGBT leaders decided to meet in February at the Hotel State (aka The Stats) (northeast corner of 12th and Wyandotte; since demolished) in downtown Kansas City, Missouri. It was here that they decided, with the Vietnam War growing, to launch a national campaign to protest the exclusion of homosexuals by the U.S. Military.

NPCHO united and formed the North American Conference of Homophile Organizations (NACHO, pronounced "NAy-KO").

Drew Shafer, Al Greathouse, and, Larry Hungerford, created *ONE in Kansas City*. The three joined 36 others from 14 organizations from across the country. Leaders of *ONE in Kansas City*, decided not to affiliate with ONE, Inc., and the local organization's name was changed to, *Phoenix Society for Individual Freedom*.

In August 1966, at the second meeting of NACHO, organizers decided to form a national clearinghouse of gay and lesbian publications. *Phoenix Society for Individual Freedom* in Kansas City was selected as the home and operator of the "Homophile Clearinghouse.

Drew Shafer led the charge on May 20, 1968, to legally charter the *Phoenix Society for Individual Freedom*. The charter for the nonprofit organization was executed in Illinois because that state had removed its sodomy laws in 1961.

Among the first Board of Directors of *Phoenix Society* were Drew Shafer; Mrs. Estelle Graham; and, Marc Jeffers. Others soon joined the cause, myself included. Among them were: Chris Gordon; Richard C. Barber; Paul R. Goldman; William Wynn; and, Dale and Donna Martin.

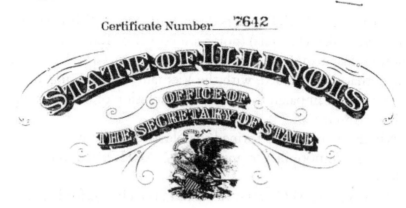

Certificate Number __7642

STATE OF ILLINOIS
OFFICE OF
THE SECRETARY OF STATE

To all to whom these Presents Shall Come, Greeting:

Whereas, Articles of Incorporation duly signed and verified of

PHOENIX SOCIETY FOR INDIVIDUAL FREEDOM

have been filed in the Office of the Secretary of State on the __20th__ day of __May__ A.D. 19 __68__ as provided by the "GENERAL NOT FOR PROFIT CORPORATION ACT" of Illinois, approved July 17, 1943, in force January 1, A.D. 1944;

Now Therefore, I, PAUL POWELL, Secretary of State of the State of Illinois, by virtue of the powers vested in me by law, do hereby issue this Certificate of Incorporation and attach thereto a copy of the Articles of Incorporation of the aforesaid corporation.

In Testimony Whereof, I hereto set my hand, and cause to be affixed the Great Seal of the State of Illinois. Done at the City of Springfield this __20th__ day of __May__ A.D. 19 __68__ and of the Independence of the United States the one hundred and __92nd__.

(SEAL)

Paul Powell

SECRETARY OF STATE

We had a core group of volunteers who worked tirelessly for *Phoenix Society*. Though short lived, *Phoenix Society* had a definitive impact, putting Kansas City's LGBT community on the map.

Mrs. Estelle Graham, by the way, was the pseudonym used by Phyllis Shafer; she used the Graham signature when writing publicly, at least during the time when *Phoenix Society* was gaining national attention through 1971. Mrs. Shafer noted in one of her scrapbooks that, "Drew figured two Shafers in the group, the *Phoenix Society for Individual Freedom*, was too much like a family affair."

But the *Phoenix Society* was a family affair of sorts. Not only was Drew the leading proponent of Phoenix; but, his mother was a vocal supporter. And, his father, Robert A. Shafer, had been a pressman for Sexton Printing and also Burd and Fletcher Co. These professional associations and skills guided or aided Drew, and *The Phoenix Society* began publishing literature and reporting news about gays and lesbians.

Drew taught us the mechanics. Mr. Shafer, retired for the most part, kept old printing machinery at their family home at 1838 E 49th Street. He gave Drew one of his old presses, which was installed in the basement of the Phoenix House.

Phoenix House, our home by 1969, was located at 1333 East Linwood Boulevard (the southwest corner of East Linwood Boulevard and The Paseo) in Kansas City.

I believe it was previously owned by Dr. and Mrs. Arlan E. and Frances Vaughn. Dr. Vaughn operated an osteopathic clinic at that location before selling it to Drew. The Vaughn's lived at 1308 E. 108th Street (1966 Kansas City city directory). Previous tenants included Mr. and Mrs. Sheldon A. and Wanda Stiers (1966 directory; he was a salesman for Davis Paint); and, Ms. Stella Mattox (1967 directory).

Among the publications of the *Phoenix Society* was a newsletter that predated the organization's incorporation in 1968.

CHANGING TIMES

In August 1966, *The Phoenix: Homophile Voice of Kansas City* *(which quickly changed to The Phoenix: Midwest Homophile Voice)* immediately began being distributed at gay and straight night clubs, college campuses, and across the country by mail in brown-wrapped mailers.

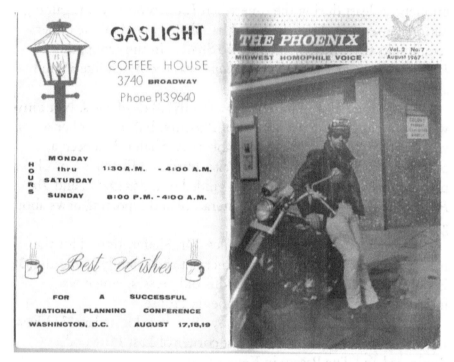

We created *The Phoenix* monthly newsletter using old linotype machines, paste-up-boards, hand-drawn graphics, and photography that we'd taken ourselves. We had to burn metal plates with which to print.

The Phoenix's costs were offset by advertising. Ads, at least at first, weren't very hard to get since there were anywhere from six to eleven gay bars operating simultaneously in Kansas City at any given time. I designed many of the ads and covers, as well as added cartoons and articles for *The Phoenix*. [Editor's note: a complete collection of *The Phoenix* newsletters are being sought for preservation.]

Before long, we got the attention of other, larger gay organizations, like New York City's *Mattachine Society*. Very quickly, *The Phoenix House* became a centralized, information clearinghouse as well as distributor for other gay magazines around the United States from New York to California, and even some international groups. Talk about monthly envelope stuffing!

It was a busy time and things were going well, until we began getting frequent media attention. Drew was the spokesperson and liaison with the media. Many within the gay community became afraid of the attention drawn to it, and feared reprisals from their heterosexual counterparts. Some of those fears were justifiable; most were not. A sharp division was drawn between those who believed we had the right to be open and be ourselves, and those who wanted to keep the protected status quo.

STONEWALL

It was now the spring of 1969.

The Italian "family" bars, then owned by John Trucillo and Joe Lombardo, started pulling their ads from *The Phoneix*, and many gays were avoiding anything to do with the pariah of the 'dangerous' *Phoenix Society*. There were, however, out of the burning fires of change, a few stalwart gay men and women who decided to try and open their own bars. It was the beginning of a new era. Kansas City gays were now becoming an independent and local, vocal voice. A few short months later, the Stonewall Riots would become the marker and song from which gay and lesbian activism would march.

The infamous Stonewall Riots took place in New York City, beginning on June 27, 1969.

I wish I could recall details of how either Drew or I first heard about or felt after the Stonewall Riots. I'm afraid I have no distinct memories of our immediate reaction. The news of the riots were on television, and because Phoenix Society became a Midwest clearinghouse for gay information between the coasts, we received a lot of updates at Phoenix House from Mattachine Society and other organizations who were involved in distributing their magazines to Phoenix.

I'm certain we were both shocked and, of course, delighted at the courage of the gays fighting back.

Wishing to be second to no one politically, the *Phoenix Society* organized marches in Kansas City as well. In conservative cities where we peacefully marched in protest, like Columbia, Missouri, we had eggs tossed at us, and we were *warned* that if we tried to march in Jefferson City, the Capitol, they would provide us with NO protection from opposing factions at all. We became important enough for people like Anita Bryant to visit, and campaign against us in Kansas City's newly built, downtown Kemper Arena. What a grand 'anti-Anita' demonstration there was that day! This was about the time when she got the famous cream pie thrust in her face during a press junket.

The local Westport Methodist Church was still one of our staunchest allies within the heterosexual community. However, it would be another five years before Parents, Families and Friends of Lesbians and Gays, Greater Kansas City Chapter, Inc. (PFLAG) was on the scene, and Drew's mother, Phyllis Shafer, became a very proud PFLAG member. Nationally, it was a turning point for lesbians as well, and they were demanding increasing recognition for their contributions to the movement. The challenge was on to make the movement one of lesbians and gays, as opposed to just the gay movement, which, at the time, implied it was run only by activist gay males.

The country—gay and straight—was changing fast...and generally for the better.

I even visited New York City in 1970, and happened to be there on the auspicious occasion to march in the first Gay Pride Parade commemorating the one-year anniversary of the Stonewall Riots. Very aware of the importance and significance of the march, and fully behind the whole idea, I marched along with the crowd from Christopher Street to the final meeting place at Sheep's Meadow in Central Park. Comparatively, it was a small parade by

today's standards, and I don't recall there were any major
'incidences.' One coincidence was that my brother showed up to
take pictures of the event, and he happened to spot me there! He
lived, at that time, in Seagate, a private community off Coney Island,
and was currently heavy into photography as a hobby.

All this change did have its consequences, and left behind
some wounded in the aftermath.

The *Phoenix Society* was falling apart. Sadly, with its
advertisement income withering, the paper could barely pay for
itself. And, it could never cover the costs of maintaining the
expenses it incurred in the large home that Drew had been
generously donating. The organization never had to pay rent,
electric, oil heating, or water. Folks helping with the organization
weren't making it easier by opening windows while the heat was on,
and leaving lights on all night downstairs.

When, after just a few short years when we had to give up
Phoenix House, the original owner was very nice to let us give it up
without suing us for breaking the lease. We just couldn't afford to
keep it going. The organization suffered because there was no place
else it could go, and no one else was willing to take up the mantle of
leadership.

By 1972, *Phoenix Society for Individual Freedom* was no more.
The organization, unlike the legendary bird, would not rise again.
Both Phoenix House and the organization were Drew's pride and
joy.

LIVING and LOVING

Dinner Theater had become the rage, and there were at least
three of them at any given time in Kansas City. I performed in those
and many others throughout the mid- and southwest for over
nineteen years. I'd even joined Equity until I learned it was too hard
to find theaters that paid union wages. I much preferred working
more often for less, than not working at all.

Drew was my constant, always backing me and supporting my theatrical endeavors. I rarely had to perform any other job, and when those dry-spells came along, he was perfectly fine with my staying home and taking care of the household chores. I loved to cook, so he ate well when I wasn't on the road. Otherwise, he'd eat out or over his mother's. We joked that "My poor baby would burn Jell-O." He eventually learned to cook Kraft Macaroni and Cheese dinners, God bless him. So, he wasn't a cook!

When I met Drew, he had been making a very good salary working in both the office and warehouse of Caterpillar Tractor Company for nine years. Shortly before I met him, he'd announced to his blue-collar coworkers and fellow union members that he was going to be on a radio talk show, but he did not tell them the topic of discussion. Curious, almost everybody tuned in and almost as immediately he was nearly fired from his job when he used his real name and 'came out' to the listening public on the radio!

Very conservative and highly incensed, his boss was livid, and did his best to get rid of Drew. However, the United Auto Workers Union told management that what Drew did on his own time was not work related, and it was his personal business. Caterpillar could not fire him! His job was saved, both he and the organization survived their first major hurtle. He would still have to deal with the stupid remarks and rude behavior from a few of his more hard-nosed coworkers for years, but he never let it rattle him. The fact is, his positive outlook and perseverance won him the respect from most all of his fellow workers.

Drew continued his regular job with Caterpillar, Inc. But, when we gave up Phoenix House, we wound up living in the basement of his mother and father's home for a few months until we were able to buy our own home together.

In 1971, we bought a mobile home at the Heart Mobile Village just outside of downtown Kansas City on U.S. 40 Highway; 2802 Circle Drive. The original mobile home was a 14' X 78'. We added a 10' X 12' extension to the living room area, half of which became his tool room. He added a fully-enclosed deck on our home, and re-did the interior of the kitchen while I was away in Albuquerque doing three shows for six months. When he wasn't at his full-time job at Caterpillar, Inc., he loved working around the house, fixing, building, and repairing.

In addition to being adept at electrical wiring, and plumbing, Drew was also a mechanic. We'd gone through a variety of used Volkswagen vehicles, including an old bus that often had to be pushed to jump-start it using the clutch. By 1973, we were doing a little better, and we actually bought a brand new Volkswagen Super Beetle.

Drew and I went through some difficult times together. Not for any lack of love and respect, but money always seemed to be illusive commodity. He'd put

115

himself in great debt over the years trying to purchase the three story home in which we lived, and to provide a location for the *Phoenix Society*. The Society's funding had little community support. When I met Drew, he was more than $40,000 in the hole (that was in 1969). By the time we lost the home, it was in excess of $50,000. The *rich* guy I thought I'd gotten hitched to was poorer than I was...and I had nothing.

It took us almost eighteen years to climb out of the pit of debt, and to finally start having a financially, stress-free life. Sadly, Drew would not really enjoy our nearly debt-free life together, because of what was to come.

THE JEWEL BOX LOUNGE

When I began to work professionally, I played some wonderful roles: the Emcee in *Cabaret*, Cocky in *The Roar of the Greasepaint...*, Nicely-Nicely in *Guys and Dolls*, Tevya in *Fiddler on the Roof*, Hysterium in *A Funny Thing Happened on the Way to the Forum*, Noah in *Two By Two*, Colonel Pickering in *My Fair Lady*,

THE JEWEL BOX LOUNGE – 3223 TROOST AVENUE – KANSAS CITY, MISSOURI

116

Fagin in *Oliver*, Emory in *Boys In The Band* and Dodge in Sam Shepherd's *The Buried Child*.

Around 1978, I stopped in on Kansas City's own impersonators' club, *The Jewel Box Lounge*. A senior performer who had been working there for years, Skip Arnold, had heard me sing and wanted to know if I wanted to emcee for them. I would come out on stage, sing a song, and introduce the next female impersonation act. It was great! Every act was live (no lip-syncing). The '*girls*' were fun, with a few exceptions, and it was easy work. The clientele was diverse and accepting...mostly tourists and local fans.

At one point, Skip asked me if I could fill in with some kind of comedy act, only dressed as a woman. I came up with a character called "Mrs. Corrie Miller," an elderly, birdlike, English matron. I would start out in the audience pretending to be a little old lady tourist who the gay boys just adored, and on occasion, would take out of the nursing home for a night on the town. Mrs. Miller was dreadfully proper, polite and saccharin sweet. But, she also had low tolerance to alcohol, and only after a few sips, she'd become 'tiddly.'

Skip would introduce me (as Mrs. Corrie Miller) to the audience as a regular patron, and then invite me up to the stage. She'd ask me what I would like to drink, and Corrie, would say, "I love pink champagne!" And every night, after receiving her glass of pink champagne (sparkling water with grenadine), Corrie would sing the only song she knew, "*Born Free,*" in a rather tortuous falsetto. After every performance Skip would find some rather embarrassing sexual 'toy' in her purse, sending Corrie back out into the audience amusingly embarrassed. I'll never forget how so many straight tourists reached out to help that 'frail old lady' off the stage!

The Kosher Ham is the tag title I used in my nightclub act at *The Jewel Box Lounge*. The act was such a hit that I wound up adding more and more characters. Through the years, I've had opportunities to either make a few bucks in a live show, or help raise money for various causes. I did dinner theater in Albuquerque, New Mexico, for a six months stint and just before I left to go home,

117

CHANGING TIMES

I did a live one-man drag show for the Albuquerque Social Club. It went over so well, they flew me down a year later to do another one.

The Jewel Box Lounge, once a world renowned female impersonation nightclub, was losing its luster. The art of live impersonation, like the vaudeville days of yore, was dying. The Jewel Box was becoming run-down and seedy with much less tourism. Some of the acts moved on or moved out. There were fewer live singers as clubs could hire pretty, young boys who would lip sync to popular songs far more cheaply than a live performer who usually needed accompaniment. I was one of the last of the vocally live performers before it went the way of drag queens lip syncing to the voices of famous singers. Disco music, strobe lights, glitz, glitter and the recorded sounds of the top rock, rhythm and blues, and soul singers became the trend of the times.

THEN CAME A.I.D.S.

To be frank, from the first day, Drew and I lived in an open-sex relationship. We both considered sex to be fun, not a vow of fidelity, nor a shackle to bind you to a person, or control someone else. In our day, however, there just wasn't any awareness of what "safe sex" was, or the need for such a thing.

1980 arrived, and with it, the gay movement had taken on a greater cause...besides social equality. An insidious disease, appearing at first to affect gay males, was to be publicly labeled the *'gay disease,'* or *'gay plague.'* We were now fighting for our very lives, as well as our human rights.

Like many others, when first hearing about A.I.D.S. and H.I.V., we, too, were convinced this was some government crap they were pulling to further denigrate and destroy the gay community. The *'gay disease,'* nearly set back the movement to the Stone Age. Amazingly, the gay community itself took on the mantel of caring for and educating ourselves. While heterosexual exposure began to rise, our numbers began to lower.

118

In the summer of 1986, I joined as a volunteer for the Good Samaritan Project's A.I.D.S. hospice. Like others, I was required to take the H.I.V. test. Drew decided he wanted to go with me and get tested as well.

Drew's test results came back H.I.V. positive. My world had changed utterly. It was the first time I'd ever seen Drew truly bleak about anything. He was very frightened and incredibly not for himself, but for me. The primary breadwinner, he was concerned for my future if he weren't around. (Actor's don't exactly have a lifetime secured position.) I'd gone from footloose and carefree, to a committed half of a whole couple. Still, I set about assuring him that he wasn't to worry about such things because I wasn't planning on him going anywhere.

Drew lived with A.I.D.S. for three years. The first year he showed no symptoms, and he was soon his old self again. During the second year, he began to lose energy and his skin was constantly plaguing him with odd fungi, rashes, and itching. Although he'd never gotten the purple lesions of Kaposi Syndrome, he was losing a great deal of weight.

He was put on AZT, the only medication available during that time and considered the 'medicine of hope' back then. But, instead of helping Drew, it was poisoning him, and he began to need monthly transfusions. He stopped taking the drug, but by then he'd become irreversibly sick.

Drew had to leave work in April 1989. Fortunately, he had excellent health benefits which paid for his care. And, though he was no longer physically working there, by union rules they could not fill his slot unless he decided to leave altogether. He had just completed thirty years with Caterpillar, Inc; he could retire if he wanted. He decided to take his retirement, and let them hire someone else. He had faced the fact he was not going to return to his job.

In that third year, constant bouts with anemia finally took their toll. Frail, weak, and on oxygen, Drew stayed in our home, and I took care of him up until his last twelve hours on September

30, 1989. In the wee hours of that morning, he'd tried to get out of bed on his own to use the bathroom. I was awakened suddenly to the noise of Drew falling. I immediately called for an ambulance. Drew was as white as a sheet, and could hardly say anything comprehensible.   My baby was 6' 2" tall, and he weighed less than one hundred pounds at that point. He was skeletal. Incredibly, the ambulance drivers would not help me get him out of the bathroom! I lifted Drew, and carried him to the stretcher. I had to threaten their supervisor over the phone with a lawsuit when the driver said I couldn't go to the hospital in the ambulance with Drew. I wasn't about to leave him alone with these same Cretins who were afraid to even pick him up! Convinced I wasn't kidding, their supervisor told them to let me ride along. It was a very quiet, but intense ride to the hospital. Drew had lost consciousness. He was so ashen. I could see the pale blue veins in his face, arms and hands.

I went with Drew into the emergency room. I gave them a list of what medications he'd been taking, and provided his medical history. How could Drew have supplied this information if the ambulance had taken him alone? After all the previous visits to the hospital, I was certain that Drew would not be coming home this time. I left the hospital staff to tend to Drew, and went to call some of our friends. Frankly, I needed a shoulder to cry on myself.

Later that morning, Drew was sitting up, transfusion pink and smiling. He asked me if I would bring him a newspaper and his slippers. "Of course I will," I told him. In Drew's mind, this was be just another day of dealing with his disease. I left to get the things he'd asked for and came back a few hours later. I was stopped at the nurse's station, and told Drew had suddenly turned for the worse. The nurse said Drew had been calling for me. When I came in, he was pale once again, and spitting blood. He turned and looked at me with a weak smile, and cried, "I am so sorry," and kept trying to apologize as though he were an inconvenience to me. It took every bit of strength I had not to let him see how sad, lost, frightened, and miserable I was feeling. If he was going to leave me, I was not going to let him die worrying for me.

Close to six o'clock that evening, at his bedside, I talked to him about letting go. I constantly reassured him I would be fine; but, not if I thought he was in pain and suffering as he was. I told him I loved him over and over again, as I wiped blood from his lips and chin that he kept spitting. I must have used dozens of hospital cloths. And, after awhile, I stopped looking to even see if his blood was getting on me.

Drew was very silent for the longest while when he looked right at me, and within his eyes I watched him leave. I closed his eyes. He had loved me unconditionally for 21 years and twenty-nine days.

Drew loved gardens and flowers, particularly roses and so, as were his wishes, I had an outdoor memorial gathering in his name in the Rose Garden at Loose Park in Kansas City. He was cremated and his ashes were spread out in a beautiful and specifically designated area of one of the rose gardens at Unity Village, Missouri.

The last movie we watched on television together was *Beaches*, in which Bette Midler sings that beautiful song dedicated to her long-time friend. Tossing yellow rose petals in the air, representing his spirit, I played Midler's recorded version of *The Wind Beneath My Wings*, at his memorial service. The lyrics were perfectly apropos to the relationship that Drew and I shared.

A couple of years later, in the movie, *Long Time Companion*, there was a scene in which one man talks to his dying lover in much the same way that I talked to Drew. When I first saw that scene I felt so invaded...as though someone had recorded everything that had happened. I must have cried buckets. Then, I realized, of course, that the same scenario was being sadly played out all over our country, and the whole world, for that matter. Torn hearts aren't very different anywhere in the world.

No one smiled so often, tried so hard to please, and kept his chin up in the worst of times like Drew did. He changed me from a cold, wandering opportunistic kid into a caring man. He convinced me that there is, indeed, such a thing as a loving relationship, and it can exist and grow between two men as well as any other couple. He taught me that love is a real thing, not just something invented by Hollywood and playwrights. He showed me, by example, the values of honesty and integrity, and to have the courage to be myself...values I'd far too often missed seeing as a child.

Drew's loss was devastating to me at that time. But, his memory and lessons live on in my heart and mind.

I had considered moving back to upstate New York where most of my family had moved, and were residing in various small towns. The decision to move, however, was forced upon me. In May 1990, an ignorant landowner knocked down part of a levee by the Little Blue River at the back of our mobile home village in order to dump garbage. He never built it back up, and a severe storm hit Kansas City. The heavy rains caused the River to rise over the damaged levee, and that created a flood. Our home was flooded and nearly wiped away. Almost everything I owned went along with it. There was nothing left for me in Kansas City.

I returned to my family in upstate New York and moved in with my mother, Lillian Marie (Hoyt) Pfleger-Chiusano, for about a year after she became suddenly ill and was diagnosed with a malignant, cancerous growth in her brain.

Mom, and the majority of my family, was supportive of the relationship between Drew and me. Drew first met Mom in 1971, at her mobile home at Lake Gerry in Oxford, New York.

Mom was a strong, giving woman. In her youth, she had a passion for fun and living and carried that passion with her throughout her life. A singer and dancer in her younger days, she passed on her artistic talents to her children, whom she raised alone.

In 1982, on our fourteenth anniversary, we had my mother come out and visit us at our home in Kansas City. I even put on a special show for her at *The Arabian Knights*. I used to do this act where I'd start off as a man, sing several songs, strip to the song, *"There'll Be Some Changes Made,"* and re-dress as a woman, and finish the show that way, changing into various outfits and characters all the while singing live with accompaniment. Mom died in July 1992.

DEPRESSION

Drew's death, the loss of my home and all of my possessions, and the death of my mother, took their toll on my psyche. I had gone through the paces of living; but, a part of me was dying as well. I'd moved to Salem, New York, and taken a job at Caldor's Department store for a brief period when I began to get weaker and weaker. I felt just awful. I could barely walk or lift anything. I assumed that A.I.D.S. was the

reason, and I was glad because I had had such strong guilt that Drew had suffered and died; but I didn't.

I returned to my mother's home, and had my blood work done. Twice. Both times the results came back H.I. V. negative. I then had to go for several tests in Cooperstown to find out what was wrong with me. I was getting worse and my legs and back were really hurting. I was finally diagnosed with Fibromyalgia, Chronic Fatigue, and severe arthritis in my knees.

Now living on my own in Binghamton, New York, and knowing almost no one, I became deeply depressed and attempted suicide. I was treated for depression, and am well into recovery.

So, here I am in Binghamton, New York. I still sing. I still draw. Every once in a while I perform onstage in theatrical productions, and sometimes direct. At this writing, I've directed David Mamet's *"American Buffalo"*, *"Blithe Spirit."* I've appeared in *"Mornings at Seven"*, *"My Fair Lady,"* and, several other productions.

I have my own personal website, www.mickeyray.com and a theatrical resource website, www.stagewhispers.net.

Life is life, and we have to get on with it.

PHYLLIS SHAFER AND HER SCRAPBOOKS

Phyllis Fay and Bob Shafer were the proud parents of their gay son, Drew Robert Shafer, who grew up and became one of Kansas City's leading gay activists. Phyllis Forney was born in LaCrosse, Kansas, on August 7, 1908. She married Robert Shafer, who was born in Lincoln, Kansas, April 30, 1909. The Shafers moved to Kansas City, Missouri, in 1945; the Forneys in 1943, or before.

Drew was born on April 9, 1936. As mentioned earlier, he "came out" at an early age and his parents supported him unconditionally.

Mrs. Shafer scrapbooked and collected printed source material on issues relating to gays and lesbians in Kansas City. She also clipped articles from across the country...and people sent them to her. Topics included the long-standing questions of gays and lesbians in the military, and their equal right to legally marry.

Not thoroughly covered in these scrapbooks, sadly, is all the work she and Drew did for the *The Phoenix Society*. Those records may have been kept separately and are not known to have survived. Shafer's scrapbooks titled, "*Gays: Changing Times*," include dated material from 1937 through 1990, although coverage is most consistent from 1965-1985. While most of the articles are in near chronological order, there are a number of un-sequenced articles (as in the case of one 1966 article about the aforementioned NACHO in Kansas City.)

The title assigned by Mrs. Shafer is apropos. As you study these clippings from the beginning, you can feel the oppression in the *way* gay-related news was covered by the mainstream media, and the *types* of news about homosexuals that was reported in the couple-three years before the Stonewall riots.

The 'gay liberation movement' arguably launched in 1965 when activists led a non-violent protest in Washington, D.C., for equal employment in government and civil service. And, a few of the earliest clippings in these scrapbooks cover this first wave of demonstration. Therefore, these scrapbooks might be considered to document the ramp-up towards what culminated in the Stonewall riots that changed LGBT history forever.

As time progressed, you begin to see through these assembled clippings more activism. The words "gay" and "lesbian" begin to replace "homosexual" in many instances. The tone and feeling of the collected articles begins to lighten and brighten through the end of the first scrapbook.

But, with the positive coverage, came negative events that garnered headlines. The shocking murder of San Francisco Mayor Mascone and City Supervisor Harvey Milk, for instance, are the leading set of articles at the beginning of the second scrapbook. More activism and coverage of equal rights dominated media coverage through the 1970s and early 1980s.

Much ink was attributed to Anita Bryant and her campaign to, "Save Our Children." With all the polarizing and hateful coverage she generated, Mrs. Shafer commented in a handwritten note that Bryant did more good than bad in the long run for gays and lesbians.

The tone or feeling represented in the clippings of these scrapbooks shifts once again when, in October 1982, the Kansas City Star reported, *"Disease Afflicting Homosexuals Reported in Kansas City."* The remainder of the collection of articles focus on the "gay plague" that was soon given the name AIDS. Many of the clippings at the end of the second scrapbook remain loose and were never assembled or affixed.

Local, regional and national newspaper and magazine clippings comprise the majority of clipped and pasted or Scotch-taped material in these oversized scrapbooks, which were recycled wallpaper sample books. To see a vibrant, ostentatious wallpaper patter as a backdrop to articles about gays and lesbians might bring a smile to some researchers. It is believed that people sent clippings to Mrs. Shafer from afar when she served as secretary to *The Phoenix Society*. It is not known when or why she began assembling the clippings into the scrapbooks. It may be possible to try and date the wallpaper samples in order to better ascertain the date after which these scrapbooks began to be assembled.

Occasionally, there are programs (primarily from the Metropolitan Community Church of Kansas City, which both Mr. and Mrs. Robert and Phyllis Shafer were founding members. After much investigation of items pasted throughout, one can detail the origin and evolution of this inclusive Kansas City ministry's impact on the community. There are several invitations to Holy Unions or other commitment ceremonies that Shafer collected from congregants at MCC-KC. There are a couple of transcripts of speeches by Mrs. Shafer. Then, too, are her many handwritten notes throughout that comment to the reader to be sure and pay attention to one article or another...or, to add commentary about the validity of one article, or point out the sanctimonious nature of another article.

These scrapbooks also provide, perhaps, the most comprehensive collection of "Ann Landers" columns related to gay and lesbian issues. They run throughout, and the first dated one appears from 1950 when Landers provides advice to a "Shattered Mother-in-Law" whose daughter's husband, after six months of marriage, had had no physical interest in her. Landers wrote, *"The chances for 'curing' a homosexual are slim, even when the sick one wants desperately to live a normal life."* She pushed for an annulment. Only a small selection of less than a handful of clippings was found for Landers' sister's column, "Abigail Van Buren." And, there was an article or two from a lesser known syndicated columnist, Dr. Molner, who proclaimed in 1950 that "overindulgence or overprotectiveness on the part of the mother may be a factor in homosexual tendencies."

Of the very few references to Mrs. Shafer and her son, Drew—other than a couple of well-publicized 1977 protest marches in which they took part in Columbia and Kansas City, Missouri—is the announcement of Bob and Phyllis Shafer's Re-Marriage on May 10, 1981, at the MCC Church.

Mr. Shafer died on March 15, 1992. Mrs. Shafer died on November 24, 1993. Like Drew, they, too, were cremated.

GLAMA

These scrapbooks are just two of the many hundreds of items that have been donated since December 2009 with the creation of the Gay and Lesbian Archive of Mid-America (GLAMA), described in a following article.

MICKEY RAY BIOGRAPHY

"Coming out" was very risky, back in the days when I was coming-of-age in the 1960s. Most members involved in the *Phoenix Society for Individual Freedom*, used pseudonyms. There had been much older homophile organizations, of course; but, most of them were on the east or west coasts in large cities that were more accepting and where it was easier to be somewhat invisible. In the 'Bible Belt' of Missouri, it was much more difficult.

I also changed my name; but, not out of fear. I was 23 years old and had come out at age 16. I was young, carefree, and although I wasn't effete or displayed any of the typical 'signs' of being gay, I had little concern about others knowing if I was or not. Another

127

reason I changed my name was that I had issues with my father and chose not to carry his last name. Besides, his last name is a fright to pronounce correctly anyway.

That's when I chose the name, Mickey Ray. Mickey, a more familiar term for Michael, and Ray, which was my sister's married name at the time. They sounded good together. It has been my name ever since, and I use it for all my creative aspects from Equity acting in theater, to puppeteering, artwork, and writing.

Find out more on my website, mickeyray.com.

Mickey Ray

CHAPTER 3

Remembering *The Jewel Box Lounge*

By David W. Jackson

Who remembers enjoying a wild night on the town at The Jewel Box in Kansas City? My grandparents told me that they went there often in the 1960s. They even took out-of-town company for the hilarity of the performances. My grandfather said once they were sitting at table fairly close to the front and one of the "femme-mimics" was really poking fun at his brother-in-law. Grandpa leaned over and asked Uncle George if he wanted to go, and George said, "Heck no. I'm having a blast." Truman Capote hung out at the Jewel Box when he was in Kansas researching for his book *In Cold Blood*.

Jewel Box featured cross-dressing "femme-mimics," or female impersonators who sang songs live, performed originally created comedy and improv routines, and some who were "exotic dancers." Many of the entertainers toured, performing at night clubs across the country. Others

BOTTOM ROW
LEFT TO RIGHT
JOEY BLOCK
BUTCH ELLIS
JAMIE GREENEY
MEMBERS
A.G.V.A.

TOP ROW
LEFT TO RIGHT
CAREY DAVIS
SKIP ARNOLD
G. G. ALLEN
MEMBERS
A.G.V.A.

came to town from afar, from places like the Jewel Box Revue in New York.

Originally at the 3200 block of Troost Avenue were three clubs collectively known as "Mid-America's Greatest Fun-Complex." They included: 1) The Yum Yum Club Room, 2) Cat Ballou and 3) The Jewel Box Lounge, once called McKissick's Jewel Box Lounge, was advertised at 3223 Troost. It was later listed at 3219 Troost, the owner, John N. Trucillo/Tuccillo/Trusello) . Later, the Jewel Box moved to 3110 Main where live performances of female impersonators were replaced by lip-synching "drag queens."

Grandpa told me a story about of one of the most renowned Jewel Box performers, Rae (Ray) Bourbon, who had at least 18 vinyl records to his credit, including one that was recorded live at the Jewel Box. Bourbon's, "A Trick Ain't Always a Treat," is a hoot!

Bourbon's life ended tragically. He was convicted of masterminding the murder of a Texas kennel owner (whom Bourbon had accused of abusing his animas). Bourbon died in prison at the age of 78 in 1971.

Here's a partial list of the talent advertised over time at The Jewel Box Lounge. Those gentlemen noted with asterisks (*) are known to be alive as of this printing (2011). Mickey Ray and Bruce E. Winter are two that have shared their stories and/or materials with GLAMA for posterity. Help find these fellas so we can document their lives for posterity; we're not getting any younger!

Mr. G. G. Allen
Mr. Skip Arnold
Mr. Tommy Baker
Mr. Beebe
Mr. Rosalie Bell
Mr. Bobbie Bene't
Mr. Joey Block
Mr. Rae (Ray) Bourbon
Mr. Scottie Carlyle

Mr. Billy Carrol
Mr. George Cauden (aka Tommy Temple)
Mr. Buddy Chris
Mr. Peggy Clark
Mr. Carey (Carrie) Davis
Mr. Jamie Eden
Mr. Butch Ellis
Mr. Gene Evol
Mr. Freddie Gibson
Mr. Jamie Greeney
Mr. Harvey
Mr. Rickie Jade
Mr. Sandy Kay*
Mr. Terry Kaye
Mr. Roby Landers
Mr. Candy Lee
Mr. Terry Lee
Mr. Ty Lindstrom
Mr. Eddie Lynn
Mr. Gary Lynn
Mr. Fred Murio
Mr. Criss Noel
Mr. Mickey Ray*
Mr. Salome
Mr. Nikki St. Cyr
Mr. Timmy Saxton
Mr. Ronnie Summers
Mr. Just Tempest
Mr. Tommy Temple (see George Cauden)
Mr. Sammy Tucker
Mr. Ellen White
Mr. Bruce E. Winter (aka Melinda Ryder)*
Mr. Don Winters

CHANGING TIMES

CHAPTER 4

About the Gay and Lesbian Archive of Mid-America (GLAMA)

It's a great idea that's had fits and starts over the years. But, it's REALLY happening, now!

Kansas City area archivists and curators from the Jackson County Historical Society, LaBudde Special Collections of Miller Nichols Library at UMKC, and the Kansas City Museum collaborated to create the **Gay and Lesbian Archive of Mid-America (GLAMA)** on World A.I.D.S Day in 2009.

The goal of GLAMA is to assemble, preserve, catalogue, and make accessible a collection of diverse materials that document the Kansas City metropolitan area gay, lesbian, bisexual, transgender, intersex, questioning and allied (GLBTIQA) community.

The activities of GLAMA are varied, and will include: **1)** an oral history project; **2)** a collection strategy whereby two-dimensional materials; **3)** an artifact collection program; **4)** a web presence at http://www.glama.us where digitized samples from collection materials will be posted for access; **5)** Exhibitions; and, **6)** Educational Programs.

Equally important, we hope to gather personal stories of those who've live it. To do this, we are hopeful that we'll have the GLBT community's support in furthering an ambitious oral history project. We're seeking volunteers; so again, please contact us if you may be interested in either sharing your stories, or assisting us in dialoging with others to record them.

Stuart Hinds, Director of LaBudde Special Collections said, *"GLAMA has been in the back of my mind since I graduated from*

133

CHANGING TIMES

Library School in 1994. We had just lost another friend to AIDS, and I was concerned about what was happening to his papers and effects – and those of countless others in the area. Mr. Jackson and I have been discussing an oral history project for the past few years, but something always seemed to take a higher priority. It wasn't until recently that the three of us [Stuart Hinds; David W. Jackson; and, Christopher Leitch] *fashioned a concerted effort to make GLAMA a reality, and this was triggered in large part by the donation of the AIDS WALK T-shirt collection by Mike Sugnet.*

We all sort of simultaneously realized that we were in professional positions that would enable us to launch GLAMA in an organized way. And, we are thrilled with the response we have already received with very little publicity. We have clearly struck a nerve in the community. All of a sudden the things we lived through have become historic, and there is a growing sense that we need to capture that history before it disappears. That is the aim of GLAMA, and, with the help of the community, we will make it a long-term reality."

Life has catapulted and literally flown by, or so it seems, since the early 1980s...just look at the *Changing Times* timeline.

These last 30 years are those which we hope to gather more photographs, papers and periodicals.

It's your turn!

GLAMA collections are conserved at the Kansas City Museum and LaBudde Special Collections. All GLAMA-related contacts are directed to and coordinated through Stuart Hinds, Director of LaBudde Special Collections, Miller Nichols Library, UMKC, at hindss@umkc.edu, info@glama.us, or (816) 235-5712.

GAY AND LESBIAN ARCHIVE OF MID-AMERICA

CHAPTER 5

As Times Change, Where Might Kansas City's LGBT Community Go From Here?

With this respectful retrospective, it's exciting to envision where the Kansas City LGBT community is headed in the future.

Regardless of the unflattering stereotypes of what society has long-assumed the LGBT community to be, there have always been LGBT people who simply seek to live and love the partner of their heart's desire without prejudice, and in complete and total equality with their straight allies.

It seems to me that we're just beginning to grasp that a LGBT individual's daily life is <u>no different</u> than a straight individual's daily life. They each work; sleep; eat; volunteer; go to movies or out to dinner; or, spend a Sunday afternoon reading a good book like *Changing Times*. Most importantly, to me, is the recognition that a only fraction of one percent of anyone's daily experience involves SEX (the first thing that comes to many people's minds when they hear the word "gay"). So, to label and mount a social or moral superiority crusade on THAT miniscule aspect of a human being's daily experience is baseless.

Former Kansas City mental health counselor and former Methodist minister, Dr. Terry Norman, whose writings and publications are preserved in GLAMA, began to formulate the distinctions between "sexual orientation," "gender orientation," and that the word "homosexual" should be used to describe a *behavior* (i.e., a verb), and not to label a person as a whole (i.e., **no one is** "a homosexual;" but rather, they might engage in homosexual behavior ... that doesn't necessarily make them 'gay' or 'lesbian').

"Each generation of youths who come of age," said Stuart Hinds, *"Are organically changing the way society views gays and lesbians."* In

135

short, "sexual orientation" and "gender orientation" are slowly becoming more of a non-issue.

Whether you are straight, gay, or in between, the rest of the story is up to YOU to tell, to share, and to file in the Gay and Lesbian Archive of Mid-America (GLAMA). And, your participation and support of LGBT organizations and businesses and initiatives is vital to a future that promises life, liberty and the pursuit of happiness for *all* without bias or condemnation.

The *real* LGBT history of Kansas City remains in readers' minds. Unless memories are recorded externally in some way, you know where they end up. You might say, "*Who cares. I haven't done anything that extraordinary.*" I would answer, "*The extraordinary thing between you, me, and the community-at-large are the* miniscule number *who will take time to record even one memory, and then take initiative to donate it so it might be useful to someone else who follows.*"

With that in mind, I hope that you might realize that your experiences, perceptions, and actions (however *seemingly* mundane) are worthy of being recorded, saved, and shared with others (in the present, and for the future).

Be inspired by the unnumbered and unknown LGBT people who have lived in Kansas City in the last 150+ years, and imagine what their lives were like ... even over the last 50 years. *You might not need to imagine but know for sure IF each of them had just recorded one memory.* The same *might* be said about you in 2050. Will you?

Start by recording your favorite memory. Stop and make a note if you start to cover or think of some other memory, because I guarantee before you finish the first, you'll be anticipating recording a second memory. Before you know it you may have a small collection of random memories that may make up your own scrapbook of changing times. Remember the next step is to share and file them for posterity in GLAMA.

Thank you for your support of GLAMA.

We're waiting to hear from you!

CHAPTER 6

Glossary of Kansas City's LGBT Bars

Mostly bars, we've included a couple of bookstores and restaurants worth noting. Don't see your favorite, former hang-out here? If you have information that adds to or corrects what is here...please let us know so the next edition of this almanac may be more comprehensive.

In the future, we hope to add the approximate time frame each establishment operated; its primary clientele; owner's names; and, outstanding features or memories worth noting.

Contact the Gay and Lesbian Archive of Mid-America at info@glama.us. Please be sure to include a reference (whether it is from a specific printed or online publication, or a personal recollection).

Name	Location	City	State
409	409 Delaware	K.C.	MO
501	36th and Broadway (across from Valentine shopping center)	K.C.	MO
4 Seasons	Main	K.C.	MO
Angies	3601 Broadway	K.C.	MO
Arabian Nights (The Tent/Oasis)	3314 Gillham Road (where a Costco now [2011] stands)	K.C.	MO
Arthur's	5031 Main	K.C.	MO
Back Door Bar	423 Southwest Blvd	K.C.	MO
Baghdad	3712 Broadway	K.C.	MO
Balanca's	1809 Grand Blvd	K.C.	MO

Bar Natasha	1911 Main	K.C.	MO
Beefcakes	19th and Main Street (by Hereford House)	K.C.	MO
Big Mamma's			
Billie Jeans	5012 Main Street (originally Le Bistro; as of 2011 a part of Andre's parking lot; two doors north of Pegasus)	K.C.	MO
Bird's of a Feather	47th Street in Rainbow (formerly Pete's Pub)	K.C.	KS
Brass Rail	3502 Troost	K.C.	MO
Broadway Territory	3601 Broadway	K.C.	MO
Buddies	3715 Main	K.C.	MO
Buttonwood Tree Lounge	4800 Main (Board of Trade building)	K.C.	MO
Cabaret, The-first location	10th & Oak	K.C.	MO
Cabaret, The-second location	51st & Main	K.C.	MO
Cell Block	3200 block of Main	K.C.	MO
Chances R	Main (by Community Center)	K.C.	MO
Changes	2813 Main Street	K.C.	MO
Club NV	220 Admiral Blvd	K.C.	MO
Colony Bar, The	3325 Troost	K.C.	MO
Connections	See Sidekicks	K.C.	MO
Cowboy, The	63rd & Troost (north from The Landing)	K.C.	MO
Daddy's	1610 Main	K.C.	MO
Desert Hearts	Troost between 69th and 75th	K.C.	MO
Dixie Belle Complex third location	1915 Main	K.C.	MO
Dixie Belle first location	20 E 31st St (across street from Epitaph)	K.C.	MO

Dixie Belle second location	1924 Main	K.C.	MO
Dover Fox	4334 Main Street (across from the Quick Trip on Main as of 2011)	K.C.	MO
Ebenezer's Folly	River Market	K.C.	MO
Edge, The	9th off Broadway (across from Savoy Hotel) (Poindexter Building?)	K.C.	MO
Epitaph	31st just east of Main (across street from Dixie Bell-first location)	K.C.	MO
Flo's Cabaret	1911 Main	K.C.	MO
Fox, The	7520 Shawnee Mission Pkwy	Shawnee	KS
Gas Lamp	downtown	K.C.	MO
Gaslight Lounge	3740 Broadway	K.C.	MO
Grand Emporium	38th and Main	K.C.	MO
Hamburger Mary's	101 Southwest Blvd	K.C.	MO
Illusions		K.C.	MO
Ivanhoe Cabaret		K.C.	MO
Jamie's		K.C.	MO
Jeremy's (before Sundance)	3700 block of Broadway	K.C.	MO
Jewel Box Lounge (first location)	3219-3223 Troost	K.C.	MO
Jewel Box Lounge(second location)	3110 Main Street (where Wendy's Old Fashioned Hamburgers is as of 2011)	K.C.	MO
Joseph's Lounge	1022 McGee	K.C.	MO
Kabal	503 Walnut	K.C.	MO
Kenny's Corral/Korral	1706 W 39th St	K.C.	MO
KonTiki Room	19th and Main	K.C.	MO
KonTiki Room	3251 Main	K.C.	MO
Le Bistro	See Billie Jeans	K.C.	MO

CHANGING TIMES

Legends	518 E 31st (31st and Cherry; formerly Tools)	K.C.	MO
Midnight Sun	518 E 31st	K.C.	MO
Missie B's	805 W 39th (39th and Southwest Trafficway)	K.C.	MO
Oasis	See Arabian Nights		
Other Side, The	3611 Broadway (across from Valentine shopping center)	K.C.	MO
Outta Bounds	3601 Broadway	K.C.	MO
Parody Hall	River Market	K.C.	MO
Pegasus (called "Peggy Sue's")	5034 Main	K.C.	MO
Pete's Pub	See Bird's of a Feather	K.C.	KS
Phoenix Bookstore-first location	6 W 39th	K.C.	MO
Phoenix Bookstore-second location	315-17 Westport Rd	K.C.	MO
Phoenix, The	8th and Broadway (by former Old Spaghetti Factory in Soho)	K.C.	MO
Rail Room, The	11 Pershing Road (across from Union Station where Crown Center is presently [2011] situated	K.C.	MO
Redhead Lounge, The (Red Head Roussse)	4048 Broadway (The Riot Room now [2011] occupies space)	K.C.	MO
Road Runner			
Round Up	600 block of West 12th St (southwest corner)	K.C.	MO
Sebastian's	309 N 7th	K.C.	KS
Sharp's 63rd St Grill	128 W 63rd	K.C.	MO
Side Street Bar & Grill	413 E 33rd St	K.C.	MO
Sidekicks	3707 Main (formerly Connections)	K.C.	MO

Soakies	1308 Main St	K.C.	MO
Starz	3600 block of Broadway	K.C.	MO
Starz on Broadway	36th and Broadway (across from Valentine shopping center; second floor of the Chalet Building)	K.C.	MO
Sundance	3700 bock of Broadway (formerly Jeremy's)	K.C.	MO
Taps	19th & Main (northwest corner)	K.C.	MO
Ted's Bar & Grill	529 Walnut	K.C.	MO
Tent, The	See Arabian Nights	K.C.	MO
Terrace, The		K.C.	MO
Tools	See Legends	K.C.	MO
Tootsie's	1822 Main	K.C.	MO
Tootsie's	River Market	K.C.	MO
Trax	16 W 43rd St	K.C.	MO
Turtles	1809 Grand Blvd	K.C.	MO
UBU	1321 Grand Ave	K.C.	MO
Under the Starz	36th and Broadway (across from Valentine shopping center)	K.C.	MO
Varieties	3611 Broadway	K.C.	MO
View On the Hill	204 Orchard St	K.C.	KS
Wetherbee's/Weatherby's	2510 NE Vivion Rd	N K.C.	MO
Wilde's & The Other Side Loft Bar	(See Other Side, The)	K.C.	MO
Wind Jammer	1822 Main	K.C.	MO
Wind Jammer II	next to new Tootsies on Main	K.C.	MO

CHANGING TIMES

ILLUSTRATIONS

Front Cover

Kansas City's CHANING skyline, as visualized in a montage of "then" and "now" images, digitally spliced by the author. The full-color half of the panoramic image is courtesy the author, as taken in April 2010. The historical, 1940s era, black-and-white image is courtesy Missouri Valley Special Collections, Kansas City Public Library, Kansas City, Missouri, Robert Askren Photograph Collection (P35), Scout Statue, Harkins Commercial Photo Co. (barcode 10018180).

Chapter 1

3. Phyllis Fay (Forney) Shafer, mother of Drew Shafer, courtesy her nephews, Brian K. Forney and Galen L. Forney.

11. Rae (Ray) Bourbon "A Trick Ain't Always a Treat," alubm cover, courtesy, "Don't Call Me Madam: The Life and Work of Ray Bourbon," by Randy A. Riddle, posted at: coolcatdaddy.com/bourbon-status.html.

12. & 13. Hotel State (formerly The Stats) exterior and interior scenes, including one of its then futuristic "Jet Lounge," courtesy S. Noll Collection.

17. Cover of *The Phoenix* magazine, from the Gay and Lesbian Archive of Mid-America, LaBudde Special Collections, Miller Nichols Library, University of Missouri-Kansas City.

18. Phoenix House, courtesy Mickey Ray.

24. Bellerive Hotel, courtesy Missouri Valley Special Collections, Kansas City Public Library, Kansas City, Missouri, Mrs. Sam Ray Postcard Collection (SC58) (barcode 20000384).

25. Gay Liberation Now slogan/logo, posted at: inthemiddleofthewhirlwind.wordpress.com/bob-kohler-recalling/

27. *Town Squire* Magazine, September 1970 issue, with Volker Park on the cover, posted at: pitch.com/kansascity/aged-leathers/Content?oid=2196218.

29. Tommy Temple, from a Jewel Box promotional postcard, from the Gay and Lesbian Archive of Mid-America, LaBudde Special Collections, Miller Nichols Library, University of Missouri-Kansas City.

32. Kemper Arena, courtesy Missouri Valley Special Collections, Kansas City Public Library, Kansas City, Missouri, General Collection (P1), Kemper Arena, Number 3 (barcode 10004583).

36. Liberty Memorial, courtesy the author.

37. Willow Productions, as posted at: crosscurrentsculture.org/Willow/Willow.htm.

41. Sandy Kay, courtesy *Camp: Kansas City's Voice for the LGBT and Allied Communities*, as posted at: campkc.com/campkc-content.php?Page_ID=1613.

52. A.I.D.S. Walk, courtesy *Camp: Kansas City's Voice for the LGBT and Allied Communities*, as posted at: campkc.com/newsite/story/18th-annual-aids-walk-success.

53. 10th Voice crew, courtesy *Camp: Kansas City's Voice for the LGBT and Allied Communities*, as posted at: campkc.com/newsite/story/our-community%E2%80%99s-radio-show-%E2%80%9C-tenth-voice%E2%80%9D.

62. Melinda Ryder, courtesy *Camp: Kansas City's Voice for the LGBT and Allied Communities*, as posted at: campkc.com/campkc-content.php?Page_ID=1534.

65. Missie B's, from homepage missiebs.com.

66. Kay Barnes on the set for her *Camp* cover shoot, courtesy *Camp: Kansas City's Voice for the LGBT and Allied Communities*, as posted at: campkc.com/newsite/story/its-real-its-real.

67. *The Ladder* magazine cover, as posted at: en.wikipedia.org/wiki/Daughters_of_Bilitis

69. Late Night Theatre promo for "The Birds," courtesy *Camp: Kansas City's Voice for the LGBT and Allied Communities*, as posted at: campkc.com/newsite/story/bird-still-flies-high.

70. National Institute's Authenticity.org e-magazine homepage 'cover,' from the David W. Jackson Collection, Gay and Lesbian Archive of Mid-America, LaBudde Special Collections, Miller Nichols Library, University of Missouri-Kansas City.

71. Camp, June 2011 cover, courtesy *Camp: Kansas City's Voice for the LGBT and Allied Communities.*

76. Bicycle Challenge, courtesy *Camp: Kansas City's Voice for the LGBT and Allied Communities*, as posted at: campkc.com/campkc-content.php?Page_ID=1097.

80. Mario Canedo, courtesy *Camp: Kansas City's Voice for the LGBT and Allied Communities*, as posted at: campkc.com/campkc-content.php?Page_ID=%20%201322.

82. GLAMA logo, courtesy the Gay and Lesbian Archive of Mid-America, LaBudde Special Collections, Miller Nichols Library, University of Missouri-Kansas City. Also appears on page 134, and the back cover.

Chapter 2

101. Drew Robert Shafer, all images in this chapter courtesy Mickey Ray (from mickeyray.com), unless otherwise noted.

102. Shafer home, courtesy Kansas City Landmarks Commission 1940 Tax Assessment Photographs, as submitted by Ross Freese.

106. Phoenix House.

108. Charter for The Phoenix Society for Individual Freedom.

110. Cover of *The Phoenix* magazine, from the Gay and Lesbian Archive of Mid-America, LaBudde Special Collections, Miller Nichols Library, University of Missouri-Kansas City.

114. Mickey Ray and Drew Shafer.

115. Mickey Ray and Drew Shafer lamp post at their Kansas City mobile home.

116. Jewel Box Lounge exterior, from a Jewel Box promotional postcard in the Gay and Lesbian Archive of Mid-America, LaBudde Special Collections, Miller Nichols Library, University of Missouri-Kansas City.

123. Mickey Ray and his mother Lillian Marie (Hoyt) Pfleger-Chiusano.

124. Phyllis Fay (Forney) and Robert "Bob" Shafer, parents of Drew Shafer, courtesy her nephews, Brian K. Forney and Galen L. Forney.

128. Mickey Ray publicity photograph.

Chapter 3

129. Jewel Box Lounge female impersonators or femme mimics, from a Jewel Box Lounge promotional postcard in the Gay and Lesbian Archive of Mid-America, LaBudde Special Collections, Miller Nichols Library, University of Missouri-Kansas City.

Back Cover

David W. Jackson, as taken by Angie Heniger, November 2009.

COLOPHON

This book is self-published by the author. The main text is set in 12- or 10-point Garamond typeface, a true-type font.

Chapter heads Californian FB, at 18pt, and subheads are in 14pt Garamond boldface.

Endnotes are set in 10pt Times New Roman.

An index was created using Word's built-in indexing mark-up tools, and is set in 9pt Arial typeface, which is also employed in 11pt at the top of each page for the repeating title.

The author designed the layout of the book using Microsoft Word 2007. The finalized Word document was reformatted into Adobe Systems portable document format (pdf) format (viewed using Adobe Acrobat Reader), then transmitted electronically using file transfer protocol (ftp) to http://www.createspace.com.

CreateSpace is a *DBA* (Doing Business As) of On-Demand Publishing LLC, part of the Amazon group of companies.

A cover was designed by Jackson using CreateSpace's online cover design tool.

The book was imprinted and assigned an ISBN through the author's long-standing DBA, The Orderly Pack Rat, and is printed on-demand to a worldwide audience; the proceeds benefitting GLAMA.

CHANGING TIMES

ACKNOWLEDGMENTS

Thanks to Russ for encouraging me to pursue the world service I most love, and not minding the endless hours spent apart while I 'work' on the numerous local history projects and historic preservation activities that include, *or* revolve around my career as an archivist, historic preservationist, and local historian.

This compilation has been a personal work-in-progress since my two friends and professional colleagues, Stuart Hinds and Christopher Leitch and I launched the Gay and Lesbian Archive of Mid-America (GLAMA) on World A.I.D.S. Day, December 1, 2009.

Grateful acknowledgment is given to the LaBudde Special Collections Department of the Miller Nichols Library at the University of Missouri-Kansas City for allowing access to GLAMA collections, and extending permission for visuals appearing in this almanac and digest.

My hope is that readers might respond with articles and timeline-related events, activities, benchmarks, milestones, and other notable moments that have pertinence to Kansas City's LGBT history.

Thank you to those who have contributed content directly or indirectly to this first edition of *Changing Times.*

With successive editions of this almanac, may we each be impressed by and applaud the growing list of contributors to the official record of Kansas City's evolving LGBT history:

Ross Freese
Stuart Hinds
David W. Jackson
Christopher Leitch

John Long
Steve Metzler
Mickey Ray

ABOUT THE AUTHOR

David W. Jackson is director, archivist of The Orderly Pack Rat, an historical research and consulting service he founded in 1996. His childhood hobby of genealogy initiated at age 11 became the catalyst and inspiration for his future career.

He was graduated magna cum laude with a BS in Historic Preservation--Archives Studies from Southeast Missouri State University in 1993. In addition to securing a position as an archivist for Unity Archives at the Unity School of Christianity, and consulted on a variety of archive-related projects. Jackson has served as Director of Archives and Education for the Jackson County Historical Society since 2000. He is dedicated to the Society's mission to promote and preserve Jackson County, Missouri, history and cultural heritage. He fields more than 3,500 contacts annually for the Society's Archives and Research Library, where he is responsible for collecting, conserving, and cataloging donated materials. He coordinates a sizable volunteer and internship program; manages its on-site and virtual bookshop; updates the organization's website and Facebook pages; presents on behalf of its Speakers' Bureau; and, regularly contributes local history-related articles to local newspapers. Among numerous other programs, services and collaborative efforts, David has coordinated the compilation of more than 1,500 oral histories of area military veterans as part of the Library of Congress' Veterans History Project.

Jackson is editor of and contributor to the nonprofit organization's scholarly periodical, the *Jackson County Historical Society JOURNAL*. He has also written several, topical guidebooks (i.e., *Practical Preservation; These Walls Were Made for Talking: Tools for Constructing the History of Your House in Jackson County,*

151

Missouri; Conserving Missouri Cemeteries; and, A River Runs By It: The Story of Independence, Kansas City, and Jackson County, Missouri), and directed the publishing of several books through the Jackson County Historical Society's imprint, including: *Illustrated Historical Atlas of Jackson County*, Missouri (a 2007 reprint of the 1877 original with a new, full-name and subject index); *Vital Historical Records, Jackson County, Missouri, 1826-1876* (a 2009 reprint of the 1934 original with a new, full-name and subject index); and a six-year research project that culminated in a 2009 souvenir book, *LOCK DOWN: Outlaws, Lawmen and Frontier Justice in Jackson County, Missouri* (co-authored with Paul Kirkman to commemorate the 150th Anniversary of the 1859 Jackson County Jail and Marshal's Home, the oldest building on the historic Independence Square in Independence, Missouri).

In 2010, The History Press released a compilation of adaptations of Jackson's aforementioned newspaper columns in a book titled, *Kansas City Chronicles: An Up-to-Date History.*

To celebrate the bicentennial of the birth of Missouri's famous painter, George Caleb Bingham, Jackson assisted in the 2011 production of two peripherally-related books. *Missouri Star* and *Borderland Families* highlight the life and recollections of Bingham's second wife, Mrs. Martha A. "Mattie" (Livingston) Lykins.

Under The Orderly Pack Rat imprint, Jackson is also author and publisher of *Direct Your Letters to San Jose: The California Gold Rush Letters of James and David Lee Campbell, 1849-1852* (2000); *Recipes of our Past: Morsels from Our Grandmothers' Recipe Boxes* (2005; expanded in 2011); and, *Lost Souls of the Lost Township: Untold Life Stories of the People Buried in the Davis-Smith Cemetery, Kansas City, Jackson County, Missouri* (co-authored with Paul Petersen in 2011).

Jackson co-founded the Gay and Lesbian Archive of Mid-America (GLAMA) on World A.I.D.S. Day in 2009.

INDEX

Cognizant of the many, varied names that organizations, entities and events have used over time, the author tried to include each instance in the way that it was promoted at that time. Thank you for informing us of additions and corrections so our next edition may be improved.

Almanac and Digest of Kansas City's Gay and Lesbian History

CHANGING TIMES

CHANGING TIMES

CPSIA information can be obtained at www.ICGtesting.com
Printed in the USA
LVOW05s1514301014

411271LV00019B/1001/P